The Constitution of the United States of America, Extended Edition

A Complete Reference Guide with Detailed Explanations of the U.S. Constitution, Declaration of Independence, and Bill of Rights

Winston Mullins

Winston Mullins © Copyright 2024. All rights reserved.

The content contained within this book may not be reproduced, duplicated, or transmitted without direct written permission from the author or the publisher.

Under no circumstances will any blame or legal responsibility be held against the publisher, or author, for any damages, reparation, or monetary loss due to the information contained within this book, either directly or indirectly.

Legal Notice:

This book is copyright-protected. It is only for personal use. You cannot amend, distribute, sell, use, quote or paraphrase any part, or the content within this book, without the consent of the author or publisher.

Disclaimer Notice:

Please note the information contained within this document is for educational and entertainment purposes only. All effort has been executed to present accurate, up-to-date, reliable, and complete information. No warranties of any kind are declared or implied. Readers acknowledge that the author is not engaging in the rendering of legal, financial, medical or professional advice. The content within this book has been derived from various sources. Please consult a licensed professional before attempting any techniques outlined in this book.

By reading this document, the reader agrees that under no circumstances is the author responsible for any losses, direct or indirect, that are incurred as a result of the use of the information contained within this document, including, but not limited to, errors, omissions, or inaccuracies.

Table of Contents

INTRODUCTION — 7

CHAPTER 1: LIFE IN COLONIAL AMERICA — 9

1.1 The Thirteen Colonies — 9
1.2 Colonial Governance — 9
1.3 Growing Tensions with Britain — 10

CHAPTER 2: CATALYSTS OF REVOLUTION — 11

2.1 The French and Indian War Aftermath — 11
2.2 Acts of Resistance — 11
2.3 British Retaliation — 12
2.4 The First Continental Congress — 12

CHAPTER 3: DRAFTING THE DECLARATION OF INDEPENDENCE — 13

3.1 The Second Continental Congress — 13
3.2 Thomas Jefferson and the Committee of Five — 13
3.3 Philosophical Influences — 14

CHAPTER 4: THE DECLARATION UNVEILED — 16

4.1 Preamble Analysis — 16
4.2 List of Grievances — 17
4.3 Conclusion and Significance — 17
4.4 Impact of the Declaration — 18

CHAPTER 5: THE ARTICLES OF CONFEDERATION — 19

5.1 America's First Constitution — 19
5.2 Achievements and Shortcomings — 19
5.3 Calls for a Stronger Union — 20

CHAPTER 6: THE CONSTITUTIONAL CONVENTION — 22

6.1 Gathering in Philadelphia — 22
6.2 Major Debates and Compromises — 23
6.3 The Final Document — 24

CHAPTER 7: THE FRAMEWORK OF GOVERNMENT — 26

7.1 The Preamble — 26

7.2 ARTICLE I – THE LEGISLATIVE BRANCH	26
7.3 ARTICLE II – THE EXECUTIVE BRANCH	28
7.4 ARTICLE III – THE JUDICIAL BRANCH	28
7.5 ARTICLES IV–VII	29

CHAPTER 8: FEDERALISTS VS. ANTI-FEDERALISTS — 31

8.1 THE FEDERALIST PERSPECTIVE	31
8.2 THE ANTI-FEDERALIST CONCERNS	31
8.3 THE PROMISE OF AMENDMENTS	32
8.4 THE IMPACT ON THE CONSTITUTION AND FUTURE GOVERNANCE	33
8.5 LEGACY OF THE DEBATES	33

CHAPTER 9: INTRODUCING THE FIRST TEN AMENDMENTS — 35

9.1 PROTECTING INDIVIDUAL LIBERTIES	35
9.2 AMENDMENT BY AMENDMENT	35

CHAPTER 10: THE IMPACT ON AMERICAN SOCIETY — 39

10.1 EARLY INTERPRETATIONS	39
10.2 ONGOING RELEVANCE OF THE BILL OF RIGHTS	39
10.3 SHAPING AMERICAN LEGAL AND SOCIAL THOUGHT	41
10.4 THE CONSTITUTION'S ROLE TODAY	41
10.5 GLOBAL INFLUENCE	42

CHAPTER 11: SIGNIFICANT AMENDMENTS BEYOND THE BILL OF RIGHTS — 43

11.1 CIVIL WAR AMENDMENTS	43
11.2 PROGRESSIVE ERA CHANGES	44
11.3 MODERN AMENDMENTS	45
11.4 PROCESS AND DEBATES	46

CHAPTER 12: THE AMENDMENT PROCESS — 47

12.1 HOW AMENDMENTS ARE MADE	47
12.2 NOTABLE PROPOSED AMENDMENTS	48
12.3 THE LIVING CONSTITUTION	49

CHAPTER 13: THE ROLE OF THE SUPREME COURT — 51

13.1 ESTABLISHMENT AND CONSTITUTIONAL BASIS	51
13.2 JUDICIAL REVIEW AND MARBURY V. MADISON	51
13.3 LANDMARK CASES SHAPING CONSTITUTIONAL LAW	52
13.4 THE SUPREME COURT'S INFLUENCE ON AMERICAN SOCIETY	53
13.5 THE SUPREME COURT'S FUNCTIONING AND COMPOSITION	54

CHAPTER 14: CONSTITUTIONAL INTERPRETATION METHODS — 55

- 14.1 Introduction to Constitutional Interpretation — 55
- 14.2 Textualism — 55
- 14.3 Originalism — 55
- 14.4 Living Constitutionalism — 56
- 14.5 Doctrinalism (Stare Decisis) — 56
- 14.6 Structuralism — 57
- 14.7 Pragmatism — 57
- 14.8 Ethical Interpretation — 57
- 14.9 Debates and Implications — 58

CHAPTER 15: ONGOING CONSTITUTIONAL DEBATES — 59

- 15.1 The Second Amendment and Gun Control — 59
- 15.2 First Amendment in the Digital Age — 59
- 15.3 Privacy Rights and Surveillance — 60
- 15.4 Federalism and States' Rights — 60
- 15.5 Electoral College and Voting Rights — 61
- 15.6 Supreme Court Composition and Tenure — 62
- 15.7 The Role of Money in Politics — 62
- 15.8 Equal Rights Amendment and Gender Equality — 63
- 15.9 Immigration and Constitutional Rights — 63

CHAPTER 16: THE CONSTITUTION'S GLOBAL INFLUENCE — 64

- 16.1 The Spread of Constitutionalism — 64
- 16.2 Core Principles and Their Global Adoption — 64
- 16.3 Case Studies of Constitutional Influence — 65
- 16.4 The Constitution and International Law — 66
- 16.5 Adaptations and Divergences — 66
- 16.6 Critiques and Challenges of Constitutional Transplants — 67
- 16.7 The Constitution in the Modern Global Context — 67

CHAPTER 17: CIVIC RESPONSIBILITY — 69

- 17.1 Understanding Civic Responsibility — 69
- 17.2 The Role of Voting — 69
- 17.3 Jury Duty and the Judicial System — 70
- 17.4 Obeying Laws and Paying Taxes — 71
- 17.5 Community Involvement and Volunteering — 71
- 17.6 Civic Education and Informed Citizenship — 72
- 17.7 Respecting Diverse Perspectives and Promoting Civil Discourse — 72
- 17.8 Advocating for Change and Social Justice — 73

CHAPTER 18: THE FUTURE OF CONSTITUTIONAL GOVERNANCE — 74

- 18.1 Technological Advancements and the Constitution — 74

18.2 DEMOGRAPHIC SHIFTS AND REPRESENTATION	**74**
18.3 POLITICAL POLARIZATION AND CONSTITUTIONAL STABILITY	**75**
18.4 THE ROLE OF THE SUPREME COURT IN FUTURE GOVERNANCE	**75**
18.5 CONSTITUTIONAL AMENDMENTS AND REFORMS	**76**
18.6 GLOBALIZATION AND INTERNATIONAL INFLUENCE	**76**
18.7 ENVIRONMENTAL CHALLENGES AND CONSTITUTIONAL RIGHTS	**76**
18.8 EDUCATION AND CIVIC ENGAGEMENT	**77**
18.9 PRESERVING DEMOCRATIC IDEALS	**77**

APPENDIX A: FULL TEXT OF THE DECLARATION OF INDEPENDENCE — **78**

APPENDIX B: FULL TEXT OF THE UNITED STATES CONSTITUTION — **83**

APPENDIX C: FULL TEXT OF THE BILL OF RIGHTS AND SUBSEQUENT AMENDMENTS — **99**

APPENDIX D: SELECTED FEDERALIST AND ANTI-FEDERALIST PAPERS — **107**

Introduction

Welcome to the Journey

Welcome! You're about to embark on an exploration of some of the most significant documents in American history—the bedrock upon which the United States was built. Understanding these foundational texts isn't just an academic exercise; it's a journey into the very heart of what defines the nation and, by extension, influences the world.

Have you ever wondered how a collection of colonies transformed into a powerful nation with a unique system of governance? Or how ideas penned over two centuries ago continue to impact your daily life? This book is designed to guide you through that transformative period, unraveling the complexities and illuminating the timeless principles that continue to resonate today.

We'll delve into the **Declaration of Independence**, the bold statement that announced a new nation's arrival. We'll unpack the **Articles of Confederation**, America's first attempt at self-governance, and understand why it paved the way for the more robust **U.S. Constitution**. Together, we'll explore the **Bill of Rights** and subsequent amendments that safeguard your liberties and rights.

Our goal is to make this journey engaging and accessible. Complex legal jargon and dense historical accounts can be daunting, but fear not—we'll break down these concepts into understandable and relatable terms. By the end of this book, you'll not only grasp the historical context but also appreciate how these documents affect you personally.

The Birth of a Nation

The story of America's founding is a tale of courage, vision, and unwavering belief in the principles of liberty and justice. It's a narrative that begins long before muskets were fired at Lexington and Concord, rooted in the everyday experiences of colonists who yearned for self-determination.

Imagine living in a time when the idea of challenging a mighty empire was not only audacious but seemingly impossible. The thirteen colonies were diverse, each with its own economy, religious practices, and social structures. Yet, they found common ground in their growing dissatisfaction with British rule—taxation without representation, restrictive laws, and a lack of autonomy.

The **Declaration of Independence** in 1776 wasn't just a list of grievances; it was a revolutionary manifesto that articulated universal principles of human rights and government by consent. It signaled the birth of a nation committed to the ideals of freedom and equality, even if the realization of those ideals has been an ongoing journey.

Following independence, the new nation grappled with forming a government that balanced power between the states and a central authority. The **Articles of Confederation** served as a starting point but revealed significant weaknesses, such as the inability to levy taxes or regulate commerce effectively. These challenges led to the Constitutional Convention of 1787, where visionary leaders drafted the **U.S. Constitution**—a remarkable framework that has endured and adapted over centuries.

The Constitution wasn't perfect. Debates raged over the extent of federal power and the protection of individual liberties. This led to the addition of the **Bill of Rights**, the first ten amendments that guarantee essential freedoms like speech, religion, and due process under the law.

As you navigate through this book, you'll see how these documents were not just products of their time but living instruments that have evolved. You'll discover how landmark Supreme Court cases have reinterpreted their meanings and how amendments have extended rights to broader segments of the population.

This is more than a history lesson; it's an invitation to connect with the principles that continue to shape the United States. By understanding the origins and developments of these foundational texts, you'll gain insights into current events, legal debates, and the ongoing quest to form a "more perfect Union."

Chapter 1: Life in Colonial America

1.1 The Thirteen Colonies
Geography, Economy, and Society

Welcome to the vibrant world of Colonial America, a period that laid the groundwork for the United States as we know it today. The thirteen colonies stretched along the Atlantic coast, each with its own unique characteristics shaped by geography, climate, and the settlers who called them home. Let's embark on a journey through these diverse regions to understand the tapestry of colonial life.

New England Colonies

The New England colonies—Massachusetts, Connecticut, Rhode Island, and New Hampshire—were characterized by rocky soil, dense forests, and a harsh climate with cold winters and short growing seasons. Agriculture was challenging, so colonists turned to the sea and the forests for their livelihoods.

- **Economy**: Shipbuilding, fishing, whaling, and trading became economic staples. The abundant timber facilitated a robust shipbuilding industry, making New England a center for maritime commerce.
- **Society**: Communities were tightly knit, often centered around Puritan religious values. Education was highly valued, leading to the establishment of schools and colleges like Harvard in 1636.
- **Culture**: Town meetings were common, fostering a tradition of local self-governance and participatory democracy.

Middle Colonies

The Middle Colonies—New York, New Jersey, Pennsylvania, and Delaware—boasted fertile soil and a more temperate climate, making them ideal for agriculture.

- **Economy**: Known as the "breadbasket" colonies, they produced abundant wheat, barley, and rye. Trade and manufacturing also flourished in bustling ports like New York City and Philadelphia.
- **Society**: The population was ethnically and religiously diverse, including English, Dutch, German, Irish, and Swedish settlers. This diversity fostered a climate of religious tolerance and cultural pluralism.
- **Culture**: The Quakers in Pennsylvania, led by William Penn, promoted ideals of equality and pacifism, influencing the colony's governance and social structure.

Southern Colonies

The Southern Colonies—Maryland, Virginia, North Carolina, South Carolina, and Georgia—featured a warm climate and rich soil, perfect for agriculture.

- **Economy**: Plantation agriculture dominated, with tobacco, rice, indigo, and later cotton as key cash crops. These labor-intensive crops led to the rise of slavery as a central institution.
- **Society**: The social hierarchy was pronounced, with wealthy plantation owners at the top and enslaved Africans at the bottom. Small farmers, artisans, and indentured servants filled the layers in between.
- **Culture**: Life was more dispersed due to large plantations, resulting in fewer towns and communal institutions compared to the North.

Colonial Diversity and Unity

While the colonies differed in many ways, they shared certain experiences that began to forge a collective identity.

- **Frontier Life**: The constant push westward into Native American territories required adaptability and resilience, fostering a spirit of independence.
- **Religious Practices**: From Puritans to Quakers to Anglicans, religious motivations played a significant role in colonization. The quest for religious freedom became a cornerstone of colonial values.
- **Economic Interdependence**: Trade networks developed among the colonies and with Europe, Africa, and the Caribbean, integrating the colonial economies.

1.2 Colonial Governance
Early Forms of Self-Rule and British Oversight

The governance of the colonies was a blend of British imperial control and emerging self-governance, setting the stage for future political developments.

Charter Colonies
Some colonies operated under charters granted by the King, allowing a degree of autonomy.
- **Examples**: Massachusetts Bay Colony had a charter that permitted self-governance, leading to the establishment of a General Court where freemen could vote.
- **Significance**: These arrangements allowed colonists to practice self-rule and develop legislative bodies, planting seeds for democratic institutions.

Royal Colonies
Other colonies were directly governed by the Crown.
- **Governance**: Royal governors appointed by the King had significant power, but colonial assemblies often contested this authority.
- **Tensions**: Conflicts arose over issues like taxation and local laws, contributing to a growing desire for self-determination.

Proprietary Colonies
Some colonies were granted to individuals or groups.
- **Examples**: Pennsylvania was given to William Penn, who established a government based on Quaker principles.
- **Autonomy**: Proprietors had the authority to appoint officials and create laws, providing another model of colonial governance.

The Tradition of Rights
Colonists brought with them English legal traditions.
- **Magna Carta (1215)**: Established the principle that everyone, including the King, was subject to the law.
- **English Bill of Rights (1689)**: Guaranteed rights such as free elections and freedom from cruel and unusual punishment.
- **Impact on Colonies**: These traditions fostered expectations of certain rights and liberties, which colonists believed should be upheld in the New World.

1.3 Growing Tensions with Britain

Taxation, Legislation, and the Road to Dissent
As the colonies prospered, Britain's attempts to tighten control sparked resentment and resistance.

The French and Indian War Aftermath
- **Financial Strain on Britain**: The war (1754–1763) left Britain with substantial debt.
- **British Expectation**: The Crown believed the colonies should help pay for their own defense.

Imposition of Taxes
- **Sugar Act (1764)**: Imposed duties on sugar and molasses, impacting merchants.
- **Stamp Act (1765)**: Required stamps on legal documents, newspapers, and other papers.
  - **Colonial Reaction**: "No taxation without representation" became a rallying cry.
  - **Stamp Act Congress**: Delegates from nine colonies met to organize opposition.
- **Townshend Acts (1767)**: Taxed goods like paper, paint, glass, and tea.
  - **Boycotts**: Colonists boycotted British goods, uniting different regions in protest.

Acts of Resistance
- **Sons of Liberty**: A secret society formed to oppose British policies, sometimes through direct action.
- **Boston Massacre (1770)**: A confrontation that resulted in British soldiers killing five colonists, fueling outrage.
- **Boston Tea Party (1773)**: Colonists dumped British tea into Boston Harbor to protest the Tea Act.

British Retaliation
- **Intolerable Acts (1774)**: Punitive laws aimed at Massachusetts, closing Boston Harbor and altering the colonial government.
- **Quartering Act**: Required colonists to house British soldiers.

The First Continental Congress
- **Purpose**: In response to the Intolerable Acts, delegates from twelve colonies met in Philadelphia in 1774.
- **Actions Taken**:
  - **Petition to the King**: Sought repeal of oppressive legislation.
  - **Continental Association**: Established a boycott of British goods.
- **Significance**: Demonstrated colonial unity and set the stage for collective action.

Chapter 2: Catalysts of Revolution

2.1 The French and Indian War Aftermath

Financial Strains and New Taxes

As you journey deeper into the roots of the American Revolution, it's essential to understand how a war fought on distant frontiers set the stage for colonial unrest. The French and Indian War (1754–1763), known globally as the Seven Years' War, was a significant turning point in the relationship between Britain and its American colonies.

The War's Impact on Britain

- **Mounting Debt**: The war was costly for Britain, nearly doubling the national debt.
- **Defending the Colonies**: Britain argued that the war was fought to protect the American colonies from French encroachment and Native American raids.
- **Expectations of Contribution**: The British government believed it was fair for the colonies to shoulder part of the financial burden.

Shift in Colonial Policy

- **End of Salutary Neglect**: For decades, the colonies had enjoyed a degree of autonomy under a policy known as salutary neglect, where trade regulations were laxly enforced.
- **New Revenue Measures**: To recoup war expenses, Britain began implementing a series of taxes and laws directly affecting colonial economies.

2.2 Acts of Resistance

Stamp Act, Townshend Acts, and the Boston Tea Party

The introduction of new taxes without colonial representation in Parliament ignited a series of protests and acts of defiance that brought the colonies closer to revolution.

The Stamp Act (1765)

- **What It Entailed**: Required that many printed materials in the colonies be produced on stamped paper from London, carrying an embossed revenue stamp.
- **Affected Items**: Legal documents, newspapers, pamphlets, and even playing cards.
- **Colonial Reaction**:
  - **"No Taxation Without Representation"**: This slogan encapsulated the colonists' frustration over being taxed by a Parliament in which they had no elected representatives.
  - **Stamp Act Congress**: Representatives from nine colonies met in New York City to organize opposition, a significant step toward intercolonial unity.
  - **Boycotts and Protests**: Merchants organized non-importation agreements, and groups like the Sons of Liberty formed to resist the Act.
- **Outcome**: Due to economic pressure and political unrest, Britain repealed the Stamp Act in 1766 but asserted its authority through the Declaratory Act.

The Townshend Acts (1767)

- **New Duties Imposed**: Taxes on imports like glass, lead, paints, paper, and tea.
- **Colonial Response**:
  - **Renewed Boycotts**: Widespread non-importation agreements hurt British merchants.
  - **Intellectual Opposition**: Writers like John Dickinson penned essays arguing against the legality of the taxes.
- **Escalation of Tensions**:
  - **Customs Officials Harassed**: Incidents in Boston led to British troops occupying the city in 1768.
  - **Partial Repeal**: In 1770, Parliament repealed all the duties except the tax on tea, a symbolic assertion of authority.

The Boston Massacre (1770)

- **The Incident**: A confrontation between colonists and British soldiers escalated, resulting in the deaths of five colonists.

- **Aftermath**:
  - **Propaganda Tool**: Patriots like Paul Revere and Samuel Adams used the event to fuel anti-British sentiment.
  - **Legal Proceedings**: John Adams defended the soldiers in court, emphasizing the rule of law.

The Tea Act and Boston Tea Party (1773)
- **The Tea Act**: Allowed the British East India Company to sell tea directly to the colonies, undercutting colonial merchants.
- **Colonial Reaction**:
  - **Perceived Monopoly**: Seen as another example of taxation tyranny.
  - **Boston Tea Party**: Members of the Sons of Liberty, disguised as Mohawk Indians, boarded ships and dumped 342 chests of tea into Boston Harbor.
- **Significance**: This bold act of defiance prompted severe repercussions from Britain.

2.3 British Retaliation
The Intolerable Acts and Colonial Unity
In response to colonial resistance, Britain enacted measures that further inflamed tensions and united the colonies against perceived oppression.

The Intolerable Acts (Coercive Acts) of 1774
- **Boston Port Act**: Closed Boston Harbor until the dumped tea was paid for.
- **Massachusetts Government Act**: Altered the colony's charter, restricting town meetings and making the council appointive.
- **Administration of Justice Act**: Allowed royal officials accused of crimes to be tried in Britain.
- **Quartering Act Expansion**: Enabled British troops to be housed in private homes.
- **Quebec Act** (often associated with the Intolerable Acts):
  - **Extended Quebec's Boundary**: Into the Ohio Valley, angering colonists eager for westward expansion.
  - **Religious Concerns**: Recognized the rights of Catholics, alarming Protestant colonists.

Colonial Response
- **Sympathy for Massachusetts**: Other colonies viewed the punishment as a threat to all.
- **Formation of Committees of Correspondence**: Facilitated intercolonial communication and coordination.
- **Economic Support**: Colonies sent supplies to aid Boston residents.

2.4 The First Continental Congress
Uniting the Colonies for a Common Cause
The escalating crisis prompted colonial leaders to convene and discuss a collective response to British policies.

Convening in Philadelphia (September 1774)
- **Delegates**: Fifty-six representatives from twelve colonies (excluding Georgia).
- **Notable Figures**: George Washington, Patrick Henry, John Adams, Samuel Adams.

Actions and Decisions
- **Declaration of Rights and Grievances**: Asserted colonial rights and denounced the Intolerable Acts.
- **The Association**: Established a boycott of British goods, creating a unified economic front.
- **Agreement to Reconvene**: Planned a Second Continental Congress if grievances weren't addressed.

Significance
- **Colonial Unity**: Marked a significant step toward cooperation among the colonies.
- **Preparation for Conflict**: Discussions included measures for mutual defense.

2.5 The Spark of Armed Conflict
Lexington and Concord (April 1775)
- **British Objectives**: Seize colonial military supplies in Concord and arrest Patriot leaders in Lexington.
- **Paul Revere's Ride**: Warned militias of the approaching British forces.
- **The Battles**:
  - **Lexington**: The "shot heard 'round the world" marked the start of armed conflict.
  - **Concord**: Colonial militias forced British troops to retreat, showcasing effective resistance.

Chapter 3: Drafting the Declaration of Independence

3.1 The Second Continental Congress
Debates and Decisions Leading to Independence

As you continue this journey through America's formative years, the spotlight turns to the **Second Continental Congress**, a pivotal gathering that steered the colonies toward independence. Convened in **Philadelphia in May 1775**, this congress was not just a continuation of the first but a decisive assembly facing the realities of open conflict following the battles of Lexington and Concord.

The Context of War
- **Escalating Conflict**: The skirmishes at Lexington and Concord in April 1775 signaled that disputes with Britain had erupted into armed confrontation.
- **Colonial Militias Mobilize**: Volunteers from various colonies rallied to form the Continental Army, reflecting a shift from isolated protests to organized resistance.

Key Objectives of the Congress
- **Organizing Defense**: One of the first actions was to establish a unified military force. **George Washington** was appointed as the Commander-in-Chief of the Continental Army due to his military experience and leadership qualities.
- **Financial Measures**: The Congress authorized the printing of money to fund the army and manage wartime expenses.
- **Diplomatic Efforts**: Despite the conflict, many delegates still hoped for reconciliation.

Diverging Perspectives
- **Moderates vs. Radicals**:
  - **Moderates**: Led by figures like **John Dickinson**, they advocated for repairing relations with Britain.
  - **Radicals**: Led by **John Adams**, **Samuel Adams**, and **Patrick Henry**, they pushed for full independence.
- **The Olive Branch Petition (July 1775)**:
  - **Purpose**: A final attempt to avoid war by professing loyalty to King George III and requesting the repeal of oppressive legislation.
  - **Outcome**: The King rejected the petition and declared the colonies in a state of rebellion, closing the door to reconciliation.

Influential Publications
- **Thomas Paine's "Common Sense" (January 1776)**:
  - **Impact**: This widely read pamphlet powerfully argued for independence, criticizing monarchy and advocating for a republican government.
  - **Resonance**: Paine's clear and compelling language swayed public opinion, making the idea of independence more acceptable to ordinary colonists.

The Push for Independence
- **Virginia's Resolution**:
  - **Richard Henry Lee's Motion (June 7, 1776)**: Proposed that "these United Colonies are, and of right ought to be, free and independent States."
  - **Debate Ensues**: Delegates deliberated intensely, weighing the risks and consequences.
- **Forming Committees**:
  - **Committee for Drafting a Declaration**: Anticipating approval of Lee's resolution, a committee was appointed to draft a formal declaration of independence.

3.2 Thomas Jefferson and the Committee of Five
Crafting the Document That Would Change History

The task of articulating the colonies' reasons for separation was entrusted to a group known as the **Committee of Five**. This committee played a crucial role in shaping the Declaration of Independence.

Members of the Committee
1. **Thomas Jefferson** (Virginia)
2. **John Adams** (Massachusetts)
3. **Benjamin Franklin** (Pennsylvania)
4. **Roger Sherman** (Connecticut)
5. **Robert R. Livingston** (New York)

Thomas Jefferson: The Principal Author
- **Why Jefferson?**

- **Writing Skill**: Renowned for his eloquent writing and philosophical depth.
- **Youthful Perspective**: At 33 years old, Jefferson brought fresh ideas and vigor.
- **Collaboration with the Committee**:
  - **Drafting Process**: Jefferson wrote the initial draft, which was then reviewed and revised by Adams and Franklin before presenting it to the Congress.
  - **Revisions**: Over 80 changes were made, but the core message remained intact.

Challenges in Crafting the Declaration
- **Balancing Unity and Individual Interests**:
  - **Regional Concerns**: Delegates had to reconcile differences between Northern and Southern colonies, especially on contentious issues like slavery.
  - **Slavery Passage Removed**: A section condemning the slave trade was removed to maintain support from Southern colonies.
- **Expressing Universal Principles**:
  - **Appealing to a Global Audience**: The Declaration was intended not just for Britain but for the world, justifying the colonies' actions on moral and philosophical grounds.

Presentation and Adoption
- **Committee's Report**: Presented to Congress on June 28, 1776.
- **Debate and Modifications**:
  - **July 1-4, 1776**: Congress debated the declaration, making further edits.
  - **Final Adoption**: On July 4, 1776, the Declaration of Independence was formally adopted.

The Significance of Signing
- **A Bold Commitment**:
  - **Risking Treason**: By signing the document, the delegates were effectively committing treason against the Crown, risking their lives and fortunes.
- **Notable Signatories**:
  - **John Hancock**: President of the Congress, famously signed his name prominently.
  - **Unity in Purpose**: The signatories represented a cross-section of colonial leadership, symbolizing collective resolve.

3.3 Philosophical Influences
Enlightenment Thinkers and the Concept of Natural Rights
The Declaration of Independence is more than a historical document; it's a profound statement of philosophical principles that have resonated through the ages. Understanding the intellectual underpinnings helps you appreciate its enduring power.

The Enlightenment Era
- **Time of Intellectual Awakening**:
  - **17th and 18th Centuries**: Emphasized reason, science, and individualism over tradition.
  - **Questioning Authority**: Philosophers challenged absolute monarchy and advocated for the rights of individuals.

Key Philosophical Concepts
- **Natural Rights**:
  - **Definition**: Rights inherent to all humans, not granted by governments.
  - **Life, Liberty, and Property**: Fundamental rights that governments should protect.
- **Social Contract Theory**:
  - **Idea**: Governments are formed through an implicit contract between rulers and the governed.
  - **Consent of the Governed**: Legitimate authority arises from the people's consent.

Influential Thinkers
- **John Locke (1632–1704)**:
  - **Major Works**: "Two Treatises of Government."
  - **Contributions**:
    - **Natural Rights**: Advocated for life, liberty, and property.
    - **Right to Revolution**: If a government fails to protect

rights, people have the right to alter or abolish it.
- **Impact on Jefferson**: Locke's ideas are echoed throughout the Declaration.
- **Jean-Jacques Rousseau (1712-1778)**:
  - **Major Works**: "The Social Contract."
  - **Contributions**:
    - **General Will**: The collective will of the people directs the state.
    - **Popular Sovereignty**: Authority lies with the people.
- **Baron de Montesquieu (1689-1755)**:
  - **Major Works**: "The Spirit of the Laws."
  - **Contributions**:
    - **Separation of Powers**: Dividing government powers to prevent tyranny.
    - **Influence on American Governance**: Ideas later incorporated into the Constitution.
- **Thomas Paine (1737-1809)**:
  - **Major Works**: "Common Sense," "The Rights of Man."
  - **Contributions**:
    - **Accessible Language**: Made complex ideas understandable to the masses.
    - **Advocacy for Independence**: Encouraged breaking free from monarchical rule.

Integration into the Declaration
- **Preamble's Universal Language**:
  - **"We hold these truths to be self-evident..."**: Asserts that certain rights are undeniable and universal.
- **Justification for Independence**:
  - **Right to Alter or Abolish Government**: Directly reflects Locke's philosophy.
- **List of Grievances**:
  - **Evidence of Tyranny**: Demonstrates how King George III violated the social contract.

Religious and Moral Foundations
- **Deism and Providence**:
  - **Belief in a Creator**: References to "Nature's God" and "Divine Providence" reflect a belief in a higher moral order.
  - **Moral Justification**: Framing the pursuit of independence as aligned with universal moral laws.

Chapter 4: The Declaration Unveiled

4.1 Preamble Analysis
Understanding "We Hold These Truths to Be Self-Evident..."

As you delve into the **Declaration of Independence**, you'll find that its opening lines are some of the most powerful and enduring words in American history. The preamble sets the philosophical foundation for the entire document, articulating the principles that justify the colonies' break from British rule.

The Opening Sentence

"When in the Course of human events it becomes necessary for one people to dissolve the political bands which have connected them with another..."

- **Contextualizing the Break**: This introduction acknowledges that there are times when it's necessary for a group to separate from a governing body.
- **Natural Progression**: The phrase "Course of human events" suggests that such separations are part of the natural evolution of societies.

The Right to Independence

"...and to assume among the Powers of the Earth, the separate and equal station to which the Laws of Nature and of Nature's God entitle them..."

- **Equality Among Nations**: Asserts that the colonies have the right to exist as an independent nation, equal to other established countries.
- **Natural Law and Divine Providence**: References to "Laws of Nature" and "Nature's God" provide moral and philosophical legitimacy, suggesting that independence is not only justified but ordained.

Respecting Global Opinion

"...a decent respect to the opinions of mankind requires that they should declare the causes which impel them to the separation."

- **Transparency and Accountability**: Emphasizes the importance of explaining their actions to the world.
- **International Relations**: Recognizes the global community and the need to justify the break diplomatically.

Self-Evident Truths

"We hold these truths to be self-evident, that all men are created equal..."

- **Universal Equality**: Asserts that equality is an obvious truth, a radical idea at the time.
- **Foundation for Rights**: Establishes the baseline from which all other rights are derived.

Unalienable Rights

"...that they are endowed by their Creator with certain unalienable Rights, that among these are Life, Liberty and the pursuit of Happiness."

- **Natural Rights**: Rights that cannot be taken away because they are inherent to human beings.
- **"Pursuit of Happiness"**: A unique inclusion by Jefferson, expanding the traditional "life, liberty, and property" to a broader concept of personal fulfillment.

Purpose of Government

"That to secure these rights, Governments are instituted among Men, deriving their just powers from the consent of the governed..."

- **Social Contract**: Government's legitimacy comes from the people's consent, not divine right or heredity.
- **Protecting Rights**: The primary role of government is to safeguard these unalienable rights.

Right to Alter or Abolish Government

"That whenever any Form of Government becomes destructive of these ends, it is the Right of the People to alter or to abolish it, and to institute new Government..."

- **Justification for Revolution**: Provides a moral and philosophical basis for changing or overthrowing a government that fails its purpose.
- **People's Sovereignty**: Reinforces that ultimate authority rests with the populace.

Prudence and Caution

"Prudence, indeed, will dictate that Governments long established should not be changed for light and transient causes..."

- **Reasoned Action**: Acknowledges that revolution is serious and should not be undertaken hastily.
- **Historical Pattern**: People are more likely to endure suffering than to revolt unless absolutely necessary.

Long Train of Abuses
"...but when a long train of abuses and usurpations...evinces a design to reduce them under absolute Despotism, it is their right, it is their duty, to throw off such Government..."
- **Moral Obligation**: Suggests that not only is it a right, but a duty to oppose tyrannical rule.
- **Evidence of Tyranny**: Sets the stage for listing specific grievances against King George III.

4.2 List of Grievances
Specific Complaints Against King George III
In this section, the Declaration transitions from philosophical principles to concrete examples of how the British Crown has violated the colonies' rights. Understanding these grievances helps you see the colonists' perspective and the justification for independence.

Categories of Grievances
1. **Abuse of Executive Power**
   - **Refusal to Assent to Laws**: The King has blocked necessary legislation.
   - **Dissolving Representative Bodies**: Eliminated colonial legislatures that opposed his policies.
   - **Obstructing Justice**: Prevented the establishment of fair judiciary systems.
2. **Interference with Colonial Self-Governance**
   - **Imposing Taxes Without Consent**: Enacted taxes without colonial representation in Parliament.
   - **Quartering Troops**: Required colonists to house British soldiers.
   - **Cutting Off Trade**: Restricted the colonies' ability to trade freely with other nations.
3. **Military Aggression**
   - **Keeping Standing Armies**: Maintained armies in peacetime without consent.
   - **Protecting Troops from Punishment**: Shielded British soldiers from accountability for crimes against colonists.
   - **Waging War Against the Colonies**: Engaged in acts of war, including burning towns and attacking civilians.
4. **Denial of Legal Rights**
   - **Depriving Trial by Jury**: Denied the colonists traditional English legal protections.
   - **Transporting for Trial**: Sent colonists accused of crimes to Britain for trial, undermining local justice.
5. **Incitement and Manipulation**
   - **Inciting Domestic Insurrections**: Encouraged slave rebellions and Native American attacks against colonists.
   - **Hiring Mercenaries**: Used foreign soldiers to oppress the colonists.

Language and Tone
- **Repeated Use of "He Has..."**: Emphasizes the King's personal responsibility for these transgressions.
- **Building a Case**: The list systematically demonstrates a pattern of abuse, painting the King as a tyrant unfit to rule free people.

Final Attempts at Redress
"In every stage of these Oppressions We have Petitioned for Redress in the most humble terms..."
- **Efforts for Peace**: Highlights that the colonists sought solutions through proper channels.
- **Dismissal by the Crown**: The King's repeated disregard for petitions justified the decision to separate.

4.3 Conclusion and Significance
The Assertion of Sovereignty and Its Global Impact
The concluding paragraphs of the Declaration bring together the philosophical foundations and specific grievances to make a definitive statement of independence.

Formal Declaration
"We, therefore, the Representatives of the United States of America...do, in the Name, and by Authority of the good People of these Colonies, solemnly publish and declare..."
- **Unity and Authority**: The use of "We" and "Representatives" signifies collective action on behalf of the people.
- **Naming the Nation**: Refers to the "United States of America," solidifying a new national identity.

Claims of Independence
"...that these United Colonies are, and of Right ought to be Free and Independent States..."
- **Sovereign Status**: Asserts that the colonies are no longer subject to British rule.
- **Powers of Independent States**: Claims the right to levy war, conclude peace, contract alliances, establish commerce, and perform all other acts and things independent states may of right do.

Reliance on Divine Providence
"...with a firm reliance on the protection of Divine Providence, we mutually pledge to each other our Lives, our Fortunes and our sacred Honor."
- **Commitment and Sacrifice**: Acknowledges the gravity of their actions and the risks involved.
- **Moral Certainty**: Expresses confidence that their cause is just and supported by a higher power.

Global Significance
- **Inspiration for Other Nations**: The Declaration's ideals have influenced numerous movements worldwide, promoting democracy and human rights.
- **Universal Principles**: By framing their cause in terms of universal rights, the colonists connected their struggle to a broader human quest for freedom.

4.4 Impact of the Declaration
How It Shaped National Identity and Inspired Movements Worldwide
The Declaration of Independence did more than announce a political separation; it articulated a vision of human rights and government that has had a lasting impact.

Immediate Effects
- **Unification of the Colonies**: Provided a common purpose and moral justification for the Revolutionary War.
- **International Support**: Helped secure foreign alliances, notably with France, which were crucial for the war effort.
- civic responsibility.

Formation of American Identity
- **Shared Ideals**: Established values like liberty, equality, and democracy as foundational to American identity.
- **Civic Religion**: The Declaration became a symbol of national pride and a touchstone for civic education.

Legal and Constitutional Influence
- **State Constitutions**: Many states incorporated its principles into their own constitutions.
- **The U.S. Constitution and Bill of Rights**: While the Declaration is not a governing document, its ideals influenced the framing of these foundational texts.

Long-Term Social Movements
- **Abolition of Slavery**: Abolitionists cited the Declaration's assertion that "all men are created equal" to argue against slavery.
- **Women's Rights Movement**: Leaders like Elizabeth Cady Stanton drew on the Declaration's language to advocate for women's suffrage.
- **Civil Rights Movement**: Martin Luther King Jr. referenced the Declaration in his fight for racial equality.

Global Influence
- **French Revolution**: The Declaration of the Rights of Man and of the Citizen (1789) was influenced by the American Declaration.
- **Decolonization Movements**: Nations in Latin America, Africa, and Asia drew inspiration for their own declarations of independence.
- **Universal Declaration of Human Rights (1948)**: Echoes the principles first articulated in the Declaration.

Enduring Relevance
- **Guiding Principles**: Continues to serve as a moral compass for evaluating laws and government actions.
- **Educational Importance**: Studied as a critical document in understanding democratic values and

Chapter 5: The Articles of Confederation

5.1 America's First Constitution
Structure and Provisions of the Articles

As you continue this journey through the founding of the United States, it's essential to explore the nation's first attempt at a unified government: the **Articles of Confederation**. Adopted by the Second Continental Congress in 1777 and ratified by all thirteen states by 1781, the Articles served as the initial constitution that guided the fledgling nation through the latter part of the Revolutionary War and its immediate aftermath.

Background and Adoption
- **Need for Unity**: During the Revolution, the colonies recognized the necessity of a coordinated effort against Britain.
- **Drafting the Articles**: Led by **John Dickinson**, a committee crafted the Articles to establish a national government while preserving the sovereignty of the individual states.
- **Ratification Challenges**: Disputes over western land claims delayed ratification until states like Virginia ceded their claims to the national government.

Confederation Defined
- **Loose Union**: The Articles created a "firm league of friendship" among the states rather than a strong centralized government.
- **State Sovereignty**: Each state retained its "sovereignty, freedom, and independence," with powers not expressly delegated to the national government.

Structure of Government
- **Unicameral Legislature**: The government consisted of a single-chamber Congress where each state had one vote, regardless of size or population.
- **No Executive Branch**: There was no separate executive to enforce laws; executive functions were carried out by committees of Congress.
- **No National Judiciary**: The Articles did not establish a federal court system; disputes between states were resolved by Congress.

Powers Granted to Congress
- **War and Peace**: Authority to declare war, make peace, and conduct foreign affairs.
- **Treaties and Alliances**: Power to enter into treaties and alliances with other nations.
- **Indian Affairs**: Responsibility for managing relationships with Native American tribes.
- **Postal Service**: Establishment and regulation of a national postal system.
- **Weights and Measures**: Authority to standardize measurements across states.
- **Borrowing Money**: Ability to borrow funds and issue bills of credit.

Limitations of Congress
- **No Taxation Power**: Congress could not levy taxes; it could only request funds from states, which often went unpaid.
- **No Regulation of Commerce**: Lacked the authority to regulate interstate or foreign trade, leading to economic disputes and competition among states.
- **Amendment Process**: Required unanimous consent from all thirteen states for any amendments, making changes nearly impossible.

State Obligations
- **Compliance with Acts of Congress**: States were expected to follow the decisions made by Congress.
- **Mutual Defense**: Agreed to defend each other against attacks.
- **Full Faith and Credit**: Recognized the laws, records, and judicial proceedings of other states.

Significance of the Articles
- **Foundation for Unity**: Provided a framework for national cooperation during the war.
- **Symbol of Sovereignty**: Asserted the United States as an entity capable of engaging with foreign nations.

5.2 Achievements and Shortcomings
The Northwest Ordinance and Challenges Faced

While the Articles of Confederation had notable weaknesses, they also led to significant accomplishments, particularly in the management of western territories.

Key Achievements
The Land Ordinance of 1785

- **Surveying and Selling Land**: Established a standardized system for surveying land in the western territories.
- **Township System**: Divided land into townships of six miles square, further subdivided into 36 sections of 640 acres each.
- **Education Provision**: Set aside one section per township (Section 16) to fund public education.

The Northwest Ordinance of 1787
- **Governance of Territories**: Provided a framework for governing the Northwest Territory (areas north of the Ohio River and east of the Mississippi River).
- **Path to Statehood**:
  - **Territorial Stage**: Congress appointed a governor and judges.
  - **Population Milestones**:
    - **5,000 Free Male Inhabitants**: Could elect a territorial legislature.
    - **60,000 Free Inhabitants**: Could draft a state constitution and apply for statehood.
- **Rights Guaranteed**:
  - **Civil Liberties**: Freedom of religion, right to trial by jury, and due process.
  - **Prohibition of Slavery**: Banned slavery in the Northwest Territory, setting a precedent for future territories.

Diplomatic Successes
- **Treaty of Paris (1783)**: Under the Articles, the United States negotiated the end of the Revolutionary War, gaining favorable terms from Britain.
- **Foreign Relations**: Established diplomatic recognition and trade agreements with other nations.

Major Shortcomings
Economic Disarray
- **War Debt**: The national government struggled to repay debts from the Revolutionary War due to the inability to tax.
- **Currency Issues**:
  - **Continental Currency**: Overprinted during the war, leading to severe inflation ("Not worth a Continental").
  - **State Currencies**: States issued their own money, causing confusion and devaluation.
- **Trade Barriers**:
  - **Interstate Commerce**: States imposed tariffs on each other's goods, hindering trade.
  - **Foreign Trade**: Lack of a unified trade policy weakened negotiations with other nations.

Lack of Central Authority
- **Enforcement of Laws**: Without an executive branch, Congress had no means to enforce its decisions.
- **Military Weakness**:
  - **No Standing Army**: Relied on state militias, making national defense disjointed.
  - **Border Conflicts**: Inability to protect frontier settlements from Native American attacks or foreign encroachments.

Diplomatic Challenges
- **British Presence**: Britain maintained forts in the Northwest Territory, violating the Treaty of Paris, but the U.S. lacked the power to force their withdrawal.
- **Spanish Control of Mississippi River**:
  - **Access Denied**: Spain closed the river to American navigation, impacting western farmers.
  - **Inadequate Response**: The government was powerless to negotiate effectively.

Internal Unrest
- **Economic Hardships**: High debts and taxes led to widespread discontent among farmers and veterans.
- **Civil Unrest**: Incidents like Shays' Rebellion highlighted the government's inability to maintain order.

5.3 Calls for a Stronger Union
Economic Turmoil and Shays' Rebellion
The weaknesses of the Articles of Confederation became increasingly apparent, leading to calls for a stronger national government capable of addressing the young nation's challenges.

Economic Turmoil
- **Post-War Depression**: The economy suffered from disrupted trade and lack of hard currency.
- **Debt Crisis**:
  - **Foreign and Domestic Debts**: The government owed money to foreign creditors and American soldiers who had not been paid.
  - **State Debts**: States had their own debts, leading to high taxes and financial strain on citizens.
- **Trade Disputes**:
  - **Protectionist Policies**: States imposed tariffs and trade restrictions against each other.
  - **Lack of Uniform Policy**: Hindered the development of a cohesive national economy.

Shays' Rebellion (1786-1787)
Background
- **Economic Hardships in Massachusetts**:
  - **High Taxes and Debt**: Farmers faced foreclosure and imprisonment for debt.
  - **Currency Shortage**: Lack of specie (gold and silver) made it difficult to pay debts.
- **Daniel Shays**:
  - **Revolutionary War Veteran**: Led a group of farmers in protest against the government's fiscal policies.

The Rebellion
- **Protests and Court Closures**:
  - **Preventing Foreclosures**: Armed groups closed courthouses to stop property seizures.
- **Attempt to Seize Armory**:
  - **Springfield Armory**: Rebels aimed to capture weapons to strengthen their position.
- **Government Response**:
  - **State Militia Mobilized**: Massachusetts raised a militia to confront the rebels.
  - **Suppression of Rebellion**: The uprising was eventually quelled, but it exposed significant weaknesses.

Significance
- **National Alarm**: The rebellion highlighted the inability of the national government to assist in quelling internal disturbances.
- **Catalyst for Change**:
  - **Fear of Anarchy**: Leaders feared that without a stronger central authority, the nation could descend into chaos.
  - **Call for Convention**: Prompted calls to revise the Articles to strengthen the federal government.

Annapolis Convention (1786)
- **Purpose**: Initially convened to address trade and commerce issues among states.
- **Outcome**:
  - **Limited Attendance**: Only five states sent delegates.
  - **Recommendation for a Broader Meeting**: Delegates called for a convention in Philadelphia to discuss revising the Articles.

Movement Toward the Constitutional Convention
- **Growing Consensus**:
  - **Need for Reform**: Leaders like **James Madison** and **Alexander Hamilton** advocated for a stronger national government.
  - **Support from Influential Figures**: **George Washington**, initially hesitant, became convinced of the need for change after Shays' Rebellion.
- **Philadelphia Convention (1787)**:
  - **Mandate**: Tasked with revising the Articles, but ultimately decided to draft a new constitution.
  - **Significance**: Set the stage for the creation of the U.S. Constitution, which would replace the Articles of Confederation.

Chapter 6: The Constitutional Convention

6.1 Gathering in Philadelphia
Key Figures and Their Visions for America

As you delve into the momentous events of 1787, imagine a scene in Philadelphia where some of the brightest minds of the young nation convened to address the pressing issues facing the United States. The **Constitutional Convention**, held from May to September 1787, was a pivotal moment where the foundations of the current U.S. government were laid. This gathering was not initially intended to create a new constitution but evolved into a comprehensive effort to redefine the nation's governance.

Prelude to the Convention
- **Annapolis Convention (1786)**:
  - **Purpose**: Initially focused on addressing trade disputes among states.
  - **Outcome**: Recognized the need for a broader meeting to revise the Articles of Confederation.
  - **Recommendation**: Called for a convention in Philadelphia to discuss necessary changes.
- **Shays' Rebellion Impact**:
  - **Alarmed Leaders**: The uprising underscored the weaknesses of the Confederation government.
  - **Catalyst for Action**: Influenced prominent figures to support a stronger central government.

Convening in Philadelphia
- **Date and Venue**:
  - **May 25, 1787**: The convention officially began.
  - **Location**: Held at the Pennsylvania State House, now known as Independence Hall.
- **Delegates Present**:
  - **Total Attendees**: 55 delegates from 12 states (Rhode Island abstained).
  - **Diverse Representation**: Included lawyers, planters, merchants, and educators.

Notable Figures
- **George Washington (Virginia)**:
  - **Role**: Unanimously elected as the president of the convention.
  - **Significance**: His leadership lent credibility and authority to the proceedings.
- **James Madison (Virginia)**:
  - **"Father of the Constitution"**: Played a crucial role in drafting and promoting the new Constitution.
  - **Contributions**:
    - **Virginia Plan**: Proposed a new framework for a stronger federal government.
    - **Extensive Notes**: His detailed records provide valuable insights into the debates.
- **Alexander Hamilton (New York)**:
  - **Advocate for Strong Central Government**: Favored a robust executive branch.
  - **Influence**: Though his ideas were considered extreme by some, he contributed significantly to the discussions.
- **Benjamin Franklin (Pennsylvania)**:
  - **Elder Statesman**: At 81, he was the oldest delegate.
  - **Mediator**: Used his wisdom and wit to ease tensions and foster compromise.
- **Gouverneur Morris (Pennsylvania)**:
  - **Primary Draftsman**: Credited with penning much of the Constitution's final language.
  - **Advocate for Nationalism**: Supported a strong national government and spoke eloquently on various issues.
- **Roger Sherman (Connecticut)**:
  - **Proponent of the Great Compromise**: Played a key role in resolving the representation debate.

Shared Vision and Conflicts
- **Common Goals**:
  - **Stability**: Establish a government capable of maintaining order and preserving the Union.
  - **Economic Prosperity**: Create a system that would promote

commerce and address fiscal challenges.
- **International Respect**: Strengthen the nation's ability to engage with foreign powers effectively.
- **Divergent Views**:
  - **Federal vs. State Power**: Balancing authority between the national government and states.
  - **Representation**: Determining how states should be represented in the new government.
  - **Slavery**: Addressing the contentious issue of slavery in representation and taxation.

6.2 Major Debates and Compromises

Representation, Slavery, and the Great Compromise

The Constitutional Convention was marked by intense debates over the structure and powers of the new government. These discussions led to several critical compromises that shaped the Constitution.

The Virginia Plan
- **Proposed by**: James Madison.
- **Key Features**:
  - **Bicameral Legislature**: Two houses with representation based on state population or financial contributions.
  - **Strong National Government**: With powers to legislate in all cases where states were incompetent.
  - **Three Branches**: Executive, legislative, and judicial branches with checks and balances.
- **Favoring**: Larger states, as they would have greater representation due to their larger populations.

The New Jersey Plan
- **Proposed by**: William Paterson.
- **Key Features**:
  - **Unicameral Legislature**: One house with equal representation for each state.
  - **Limited National Powers**: Strengthening the Articles but maintaining state sovereignty.
  - **Plural Executive**: Executive branch appointed by Congress.
- **Favoring**: Smaller states, ensuring they were not overshadowed by larger states.

The Great Compromise (Connecticut Compromise)
- **Architect**: Roger Sherman.
- **Resolution**:
  - **Bicameral Legislature**:
    - **House of Representatives**: Representation based on population (favoring larger states).
    - **Senate**: Equal representation with two senators per state (favoring smaller states).
- **Significance**: Balanced the interests of states with large and small populations, allowing for progress in the convention.

The Three-Fifths Compromise
- **Issue**: How enslaved people would be counted for representation and taxation.
- **Southern States**:
  - **Position**: Wanted enslaved individuals counted fully for representation but not taxation.
- **Northern States**:
  - **Position**: Opposed counting enslaved individuals or wanted them counted for taxation if counted for representation.
- **Compromise**:
  - **Counting Three-Fifths**: Each enslaved person would be counted as three-fifths of a person for both representation and taxation purposes.
- **Impact**:
  - **Political Power**: Gave Southern states more influence in the House of Representatives.
  - **Moral Controversy**: Institutionalized the dehumanization of enslaved people.

Commerce and Slave Trade Compromise
- **Northern Interests**:
  - **Desire**: Wanted Congress to have power over interstate and foreign commerce.
- **Southern Concerns**:
  - **Fear**: Worried that federal control could lead to the abolition of the slave trade and harm their economies.
- **Compromise Terms**:

- **Congressional Power**: Granted authority to regulate commerce.
- **Slave Trade Clause**: Prohibited Congress from banning the importation of enslaved people before 1808.
- **Export Taxes**: Forbidden, appeasing Southern exporters of agricultural products.

Debate over the Executive Branch
- **Structure**:
  - **Single vs. Plural Executive**: Decided on a single president to ensure decisive leadership.
- **Election Method**:
  - **Electoral College System**: Established as a compromise between election by Congress and direct popular vote.
- **Term and Powers**:
  - **Four-Year Term**: With eligibility for re-election.
  - **Checks on Power**:
    - **Impeachment Process**: Provided a mechanism for removing a president guilty of "Treason, Bribery, or other high Crimes and Misdemeanors."
    - **Veto Power**: President could veto legislation, but Congress could override with a two-thirds majority.

Federalism and Division of Powers
- **Balancing Act**:
  - **National Authority**: Granted significant powers to the federal government.
  - **State Sovereignty**: States retained powers not expressly delegated to the national government.
- **Enumerated Powers**:
  - **Article I, Section 8**: Listed specific powers of Congress, including taxation, defense, and regulating commerce.
- **Necessary and Proper Clause**:
  - **Flexibility**: Allowed Congress to make laws needed to execute its enumerated powers.

- **Supremacy Clause**:
  - **Article VI**: Established the Constitution and federal laws as the supreme law of the land.

6.3 The Final Document

Presenting the Constitution to the States

After months of rigorous debate, compromise, and drafting, the convention produced a new Constitution that would redefine the American government.

The Drafting Process
- **Committee of Detail**:
  - **Purpose**: Tasked with organizing the resolutions passed by the convention into a coherent document.
  - **Members**: Included John Rutledge, Edmund Randolph, Nathaniel Gorham, Oliver Ellsworth, and James Wilson.
- **Committee of Style and Arrangement**:
  - **Final Touches**: Refined the language and structure.
  - **Gouverneur Morris**: Played a significant role in crafting the final wording, including the famous preamble.

The Preamble

"We the People of the United States, in Order to form a more perfect Union..."
- **Significance**:
  - **Unity**: Emphasized that the government derives its power from the people, not the states.
  - **Goals**: Listed objectives like establishing justice, ensuring domestic tranquility, and securing the blessings of liberty.

Structure of Government
- **Legislative Branch (Article I)**:
  - **Congress**: Bicameral legislature consisting of the House of Representatives and the Senate.
  - **Powers**: Detailed enumerated powers, including taxation, regulating commerce, and declaring war.
- **Executive Branch (Article II)**:
  - **President**: Defined the role, powers, and responsibilities.

- **Duties**: Commander-in-chief, treaty-making (with Senate approval), and ensuring laws are faithfully executed.
- **Judicial Branch (Article III)**:
  - **Supreme Court**: Established a federal judiciary.
  - **Jurisdiction**: Outlined the scope of judicial power, including cases arising under the Constitution.

Checks and Balances
- **Interdependence**: Each branch has specific powers that can limit or check the others, preventing any single branch from dominating.
- **Examples**:
  - **Veto Power**: President can veto legislation; Congress can override.
  - **Judicial Review**: Though not explicitly stated, it established the judiciary's role in interpreting laws.

Federalism
- **Division of Power**:
  - **Enumerated Powers**: Federal government's powers are specified.
  - **Reserved Powers**: Powers not delegated to the federal government are reserved for the states.

Amendment Process (Article V)
- **Flexibility**:
  - **Proposal**: Amendments can be proposed by a two-thirds vote in both houses of Congress or by a convention called for by two-thirds of state legislatures.
  - **Ratification**: Requires approval by three-fourths of state legislatures or conventions.
- **Significance**: Allows the Constitution to adapt over time while preventing easy alterations.

Ratification (Article VII)
- **Requirement**:
  - **Nine States Needed**: The Constitution would take effect upon ratification by nine of the thirteen states.
- **Presentation to the States**:
  - **September 17, 1787**: Delegates signed the Constitution.
  - **Transmittal**: Sent to Congress and then to the states for consideration.

Signing the Constitution
- **Delegates' Perspectives**:
  - **Unanimity Not Achieved**: Some delegates refused to sign due to concerns over the absence of a bill of rights and other issues.
- **Notable Non-Signers**:
  - **George Mason (Virginia)**: Objected to the lack of explicit protections for individual rights.
  - **Elbridge Gerry (Massachusetts)**: Feared excessive federal power.
- **Final Signatories**:
  - **39 Delegates Signed**: Out of the 55 who attended.
  - **Benjamin Franklin's Remark**: Commented on the sun painted on the back of Washington's chair, expressing optimism that it was a rising sun, symbolizing a new beginning.

Chapter 7: The Framework of Government

As you continue exploring the formation of the United States, this chapter delves into the **U.S. Constitution**, the blueprint for American governance. The Constitution established a federal system with a delicate balance between national and state powers, outlining the structure and functions of the government. Understanding its components helps you appreciate how it has guided the nation for over two centuries.

7.1 The Preamble
Analyzing the Introduction and Vision for Governance
The **Preamble** serves as the opening statement of the Constitution, encapsulating the framers' intentions and the core purposes of the new government.
Text and Interpretation
The Preamble begins with the iconic phrase:
- **"We the People of the United States..."**

This powerful opening emphasizes that the government's authority derives from the people themselves, not from the states or a monarch. It signifies a collective identity and unity among the citizens.
Objectives Outlined
The Preamble sets forth six key goals:
1. **Form a More Perfect Union**: Improve upon the previous system under the Articles of Confederation by creating a stronger, more effective national government.
2. **Establish Justice**: Develop a legal system that is fair and equitable, ensuring laws are applied consistently.
3. **Ensure Domestic Tranquility**: Maintain peace and order within the country, preventing internal conflicts and rebellions.
4. **Provide for the Common Defense**: Protect the nation against external threats and aggression.
5. **Promote the General Welfare**: Support conditions that benefit the well-being of all citizens, including economic prosperity and public services.
6. **Secure the Blessings of Liberty**: Protect the freedoms and rights of current and future generations.

By stating these objectives, the framers articulated a vision for a government that balances individual liberties with the collective good.

7.2 Article I – The Legislative Branch
Powers and Structure of Congress
Article I establishes the **Legislative Branch**, responsible for making federal laws. It creates a bicameral legislature called Congress, consisting of the **House of Representatives** and the **Senate**.
Section 1: Legislative Powers
- **Vesting Clause**: All legislative powers are granted to Congress, dividing it into two chambers.

Section 2: The House of Representatives
- **Composition**: Members are elected every two years by the people of the various states.
- **Qualifications**:
    - **Age**: At least 25 years old.
    - **Citizenship**: U.S. citizen for at least seven years.
    - **Residency**: Must live in the state they represent.
- **Apportionment**:
    - **Based on Population**: Seats are allocated according to each state's population.
    - **Census Requirement**: A national census is conducted every ten years to adjust representation.
- **Sole Powers**:
    - **Impeachment**: The House has the exclusive authority to initiate impeachment proceedings against federal officials.
    - **Revenue Bills**: All bills for raising revenue must originate in the House.

Section 3: The Senate
- **Composition**: Each state has two senators, serving six-year terms.
- **Qualifications**:
    - **Age**: At least 30 years old.
    - **Citizenship**: U.S. citizen for at least nine years.
    - **Residency**: Must live in the state they represent.
- **Election of Senators**:
    - **Original Method**: Senators were originally chosen by state legislatures.

- o **17th Amendment Change**: Since 1913, senators are elected directly by the people.
- **Staggered Terms**: Approximately one-third of the Senate is up for election every two years, ensuring continuity.
- **Sole Powers**:
  - o **Impeachment Trials**: The Senate conducts trials for impeached officials; a two-thirds vote is required for conviction.
  - o **Treaty Ratification**: Must approve treaties negotiated by the President with a two-thirds vote.
  - o **Confirmation of Appointments**: Confirms presidential appointments, including cabinet members, judges, and ambassadors.

Section 4-6: Operations and Procedures
- **Elections and Meetings**:
  - o States determine the time, place, and manner of elections.
  - o Congress must assemble at least once a year.
- **Rules and Conduct**:
  - o Each house sets its own rules and can discipline its members.
  - o Proceedings are recorded in the Congressional Record.
- **Privileges and Restrictions**:
  - o Members are paid a salary from the U.S. Treasury.
  - o Immunity from arrest during sessions (except for serious crimes).
  - o Prohibited from holding other federal offices during their term.

Section 7: Legislative Process
- **Bill Passage**:
  - o **Origination**: Revenue bills start in the House; other bills can originate in either chamber.
  - o **Approval**: Must pass both the House and the Senate.
- **Presidential Action**:
  - o **Signing**: President signs the bill into law.
  - o **Veto**: President can veto a bill; Congress can override with a two-thirds majority in both houses.
  - o **Pocket Veto**: If the President takes no action within ten days and Congress is in session, the bill becomes law without a signature. If Congress adjourns, the bill does not become law.

Section 8: Enumerated Powers of Congress
Congress has specific powers, including:
1. **Taxation**: Levy and collect taxes, duties, imposts, and excises to pay debts and provide for defense and welfare.
2. **Borrowing Money**: On the credit of the United States.
3. **Regulating Commerce**: With foreign nations, among the states, and with Native American tribes.
4. **Naturalization and Bankruptcy**: Establish uniform laws.
5. **Coining Money**: Regulate currency and standards of weights and measures.
6. **Postal Service**: Establish post offices and postal roads.
7. **Patents and Copyrights**: Promote science and arts by securing rights to authors and inventors.
8. **Federal Courts**: Constitute tribunals inferior to the Supreme Court.
9. **Piracy and International Law**: Define and punish offenses.
10. **War Powers**: Declare war, grant letters of marque and reprisal, and regulate captures.
11. **Armed Forces**: Raise and support armies and a navy.
12. **Militia**: Provide for calling forth, organizing, and disciplining the militia.
13. **Legislative Authority Over D.C.**: Exercise exclusive legislation over the federal district.
14. **Necessary and Proper Clause**: Make all laws necessary and proper for executing the foregoing powers.

Section 9: Limits on Congress
- **Slave Trade**: Could not prohibit the importation of enslaved people before 1808 (since superseded by amendments).
- **Habeas Corpus**: Cannot suspend the writ except in cases of rebellion or invasion.
- **Ex Post Facto Laws and Bills of Attainder**: Prohibited from passing laws that criminalize actions retroactively or target individuals without trial.

- **Titles of Nobility**: Cannot grant titles or accept gifts from foreign states without consent.

Section 10: Limits on States

States are restricted from:
- Entering treaties or alliances.
- Coining money.
- Passing ex post facto laws or bills of attainder.
- Impairing contracts.
- Engaging in war unless invaded.

7.3 Article II – The Executive Branch

Powers of the Presidency

Article II establishes the **Executive Branch**, headed by the **President of the United States**, responsible for enforcing federal laws and managing the administration.

Section 1: The President and Vice President
- **Term of Office**: Four-year terms, with the 22nd Amendment later limiting presidents to two terms.
- **Election Process**:
  - **Electoral College**: Each state appoints electors equal to its total number of senators and representatives.
  - **Original Method**: Electors cast two votes; the candidate with the majority became President, second became Vice President.
  - **12th Amendment Change**: Electors cast separate votes for President and Vice President.
- **Qualifications**:
  - **Natural-Born Citizen**: Must be born a U.S. citizen.
  - **Age**: At least 35 years old.
  - **Residency**: Resident within the U.S. for at least 14 years.
- **Succession**:
  - **Vice President**: Assumes the presidency in case of removal, death, resignation, or inability.
  - **Presidential Succession Act and 25th Amendment**: Further clarify the line of succession.
- **Compensation**:
  - **Fixed Salary**: Cannot be increased or decreased during the term.
  - **Emoluments Clause**: Prohibits receiving other benefits from the government or foreign states.

Section 2: Powers of the President
- **Commander-in-Chief**: Leader of the armed forces and state militias when called into federal service.
- **Executive Departments**:
  - **Cabinet Appointments**: May require opinions from principal officers in each executive department.
- **Pardons and Reprieves**:
  - **Clemency Powers**: Can grant pardons for federal offenses, except in cases of impeachment.
- **Treaties and Appointments**:
  - **Treaties**: Can negotiate treaties with other nations, requiring a two-thirds Senate approval.
  - **Appointments**: Nominates ambassadors, public ministers, judges of the Supreme Court, and other federal officers, with Senate consent.

Section 3: Duties of the President
- **State of the Union**: Must periodically inform Congress about the nation's status and recommend necessary measures.
- **Calling Congress into Session**: Can convene both houses on extraordinary occasions.
- **Receiving Ambassadors**: Represents the nation in foreign affairs.
- **Ensuring Laws are Executed**: Must "take care that the laws be faithfully executed."

Section 4: Impeachment
- **Grounds for Removal**: President, Vice President, and civil officers can be impeached for treason, bribery, or other high crimes and misdemeanors.

7.4 Article III – The Judicial Branch

Establishing the Supreme Court and Federal Judiciary

Article III creates the **Judicial Branch**, which interprets the laws and ensures they align with the Constitution.

Section 1: Federal Courts
- **Supreme Court**: Establishes the Supreme Court as the highest court in the land.
- **Inferior Courts**:

- **Congressional Authority**: Congress can establish lower federal courts as needed.
- **Judges' Tenure**:
  - **Lifetime Appointments**: Judges hold their offices during good behavior, ensuring independence.
  - **Compensation**: Salaries cannot be diminished during their tenure.

Section 2: Judicial Powers
- **Jurisdiction**:
  - **Cases Under the Constitution**: Authority extends to cases arising under the Constitution, federal laws, and treaties.
  - **Admiralty and Maritime**: Includes cases on the high seas.
  - **Disputes Involving States or Citizens**: Handles controversies between states, citizens of different states, and foreign states or citizens.
- **Original and Appellate Jurisdiction**:
  - **Original Jurisdiction**: Cases that can be tried directly in the Supreme Court, such as those involving ambassadors or when a state is a party.
  - **Appellate Jurisdiction**: Supreme Court reviews cases from lower courts.
- **Trial by Jury**:
  - **Criminal Cases**: All crimes, except impeachment, are tried by jury in the state where the crime was committed.

Section 3: Treason
- **Definition**:
  - **Limited Scope**: Treason is defined narrowly as levying war against the U.S. or aiding its enemies.
- **Conviction Requirements**:
  - **Testimony of Two Witnesses**: To the same overt act, or confession in open court.
- **Punishment**:
  - **Congressional Power**: Congress determines the punishment but cannot impose corruption of blood or forfeiture beyond the person's life.

7.5 Articles IV–VII
Relations Among States, the Amendment Process, Federal Supremacy, and Ratification

While Articles I–III outline the three branches of government, the remaining articles address other essential aspects of the nation's framework.

Article IV: Relations Among States
- **Section 1: Full Faith and Credit**:
  - **Mutual Recognition**: States must honor the public acts, records, and judicial proceedings of other states.
- **Section 2: Privileges and Immunities**:
  - **Equal Treatment**: Citizens of each state are entitled to the privileges and immunities of citizens in the several states.
  - **Extradition**: States must return individuals charged with crimes to the state where the crime was committed.
- **Section 3: New States and Territories**:
  - **Admission of New States**: Congress can admit new states but cannot create a new state within an existing one without consent.
  - **Territorial Authority**: Congress has power over federal territories and properties.
- **Section 4: Republican Government**:
  - **Guarantee Clause**: The United States shall guarantee every state a republican form of government and protect them against invasion and domestic violence.

Article V: The Amendment Process
- **Proposal Methods**:
  - **Congressional Proposal**: Two-thirds vote in both the House and Senate.
  - **Convention**: Called by Congress upon request of two-thirds of state legislatures.
- **Ratification Methods**:
  - **State Legislatures**: Approval by three-fourths of state legislatures.
  - **State Conventions**: Approval by conventions in three-fourths of the states.
- **Limitations**:

- - Equal Representation in the Senate: Cannot be deprived without a state's consent.

Article VI: Federal Supremacy
- **Supremacy Clause**:
  - **Hierarchy of Laws**: The Constitution, federal laws, and treaties are the supreme law of the land, overriding state laws.
- **Oaths of Office**:
  - **Binding on Officials**: All federal and state officials must swear an oath to support the Constitution.
- **No Religious Tests**:
  - **Prohibition**: No religious test shall ever be required as a qualification for any public office.

Article VII: Ratification
- **Requirement**:
  - **Nine States**: The Constitution would take effect after ratification by nine states.
- **Signing and Transmittal**:
  - **September 17, 1787**: Delegates signed the Constitution, sending it to the states for consideration.

Chapter 8: Federalists vs. Anti-Federalists

As you continue exploring the formation of the United States government, this chapter delves into the intense debates that surrounded the ratification of the Constitution. The period between 1787 and 1789 was marked by a vigorous public discourse between two factions: the **Federalists**, who supported the new Constitution, and the **Anti-Federalists**, who opposed it. Understanding their arguments and concerns provides valuable insight into the foundational principles of American democracy and the eventual adoption of the **Bill of Rights**.

8.1 The Federalist Perspective

Advocating for Ratification of the Constitution

The **Federalists** were proponents of a strong central government as outlined in the newly drafted Constitution. They believed that the weaknesses of the Articles of Confederation necessitated a more robust federal structure to ensure the nation's survival and prosperity.

Key Figures
- **Alexander Hamilton** (New York)
- **James Madison** (Virginia)
- **John Jay** (New York)
- **John Marshall** (Virginia)
- **George Washington** (Virginia)
- **Benjamin Franklin** (Pennsylvania)

Core Arguments
1. **Necessity of a Strong Central Government**
   - **Unified Nation**: A strong federal government was essential to unite the states and present a cohesive front in foreign affairs.
   - **Economic Stability**: Centralized control over commerce and taxation would promote economic growth and resolve interstate trade conflicts.
   - **National Defense**: A unified military command would better protect the nation from external threats.
2. **Checks and Balances**
   - **Preventing Tyranny**: The Constitution's system of checks and balances would prevent any one branch from gaining too much power.
   - **Separation of Powers**: Dividing government authority among legislative, executive, and judicial branches would safeguard liberties.
3. **Limitations of the Articles of Confederation**
   - **Ineffective Governance**: The Articles failed to address critical issues like national debt, trade disputes, and internal unrest.
   - **Inability to Enforce Laws**: Without executive or judicial branches, the Confederation Congress lacked the means to implement or interpret laws effectively.
4. **Large Republic Advantage**
   - **Diluting Factionalism**: In a large republic, it would be more difficult for any single faction to dominate, protecting minority rights.
   - **Diverse Interests**: A variety of interests across a vast nation would necessitate compromise and cooperation.

The Federalist Papers
- **Authors**: Alexander Hamilton, James Madison, and John Jay wrote under the pseudonym "Publius."
- **Purpose**: To persuade New York delegates and the general public to support ratification.
- **Content**: A series of 85 essays explaining and defending the Constitution's provisions.
- **Significant Essays**:
   - **Federalist No. 10** (Madison): Discussed the dangers of factionalism and how a large republic mitigates them.
   - **Federalist No. 51** (Madison): Explained the need for checks and balances and the separation of powers.

8.2 The Anti-Federalist Concerns

Fears of Centralized Power and Lack of Individual Rights Protections

The **Anti-Federalists** were skeptical of the new Constitution, fearing that it granted too much power to the federal government at the expense of the states and individual liberties.

Key Figures
- **Patrick Henry** (Virginia)

- **George Mason** (Virginia)
- **Samuel Adams** (Massachusetts)
- **Richard Henry Lee** (Virginia)
- **Robert Yates** (New York) – wrote as "Brutus"
- **Melancton Smith** (New York)

Core Arguments
1. **Threat to State Sovereignty**
   - **Overbearing Federal Authority**: The Constitution diminished the powers of state governments, risking the loss of local control.
   - **Distance from the People**: A large federal government would be disconnected from the citizens it served.
2. **Lack of a Bill of Rights**
   - **Absence of Explicit Protections**: The Constitution did not include specific guarantees for freedoms like speech, religion, press, and assembly.
   - **Risk of Tyranny**: Without a bill of rights, the federal government could infringe upon individual liberties.
3. **Potential for Despotism**
   - **Executive Power**: The presidency resembled a monarchy, with concerns over indefinite re-election and veto power.
   - **Standing Army**: A federal military could be used to oppress the people.
4. **Judicial Overreach**
   - **Supreme Court Authority**: The federal judiciary might override state courts and laws, threatening local legal systems.
5. **Economic Concerns**
   - **Taxation Powers**: The ability of the federal government to levy taxes could burden citizens and stifle economic growth.
   - **Favoring the Elite**: Belief that the Constitution was crafted to benefit wealthy merchants and landowners over common people.

The Anti-Federalist Papers
- **Authors**: Various writers using pseudonyms like "Brutus," "Cato," and "Federal Farmer."
- **Purpose**: To critique the Constitution and argue against ratification without significant amendments.
- **Content**: Essays highlighting the dangers of centralized power and the need for explicit rights protections.

8.3 The Promise of Amendments

How the Bill of Rights Became Essential

The intense debates between Federalists and Anti-Federalists led to a critical compromise that would shape the Constitution's future: the inclusion of a Bill of Rights.

The Ratification Process
- **State Conventions**: Each state held a convention to debate and vote on the Constitution.
- **Close Votes**: Ratification was not guaranteed; several states ratified with narrow margins and with calls for amendments.

Key States and Their Demands
- **Massachusetts**:
   - **Concerns**: Strong Anti-Federalist opposition centered on individual rights.
   - **Resolution**: Ratified the Constitution with recommended amendments.
- **Virginia**:
   - **Influential Figures**: Patrick Henry and George Mason argued vehemently against ratification without a bill of rights.
   - **Outcome**: Ratified with the expectation that amendments would be added.
- **New York**:
   - **Divided Opinion**: Intense debates reflected in the Federalist and Anti-Federalist papers.
   - **Decision**: Ratified after assurances that a bill of rights would be considered.

Federalist Concessions
- **Acknowledgment of Concerns**: Federalists recognized that addressing fears over individual liberties was essential for unity.
- **James Madison's Role**:
   - **Initially Skeptical**: Believed that the Constitution's structure already protected rights.
   - **Advocate for Amendments**: Eventually supported the addition of

a bill of rights to ensure ratification and promote harmony.

The Bill of Rights
- **Drafting Process**:
  - **Madison's Proposals**: Introduced a series of amendments during the First Congress in 1789.
  - **Congressional Approval**: Twelve amendments were approved by Congress and sent to the states.
- **Ratification**:
  - **Adoption**: Ten amendments were ratified by the required number of states by 1791.
- **Content of the Bill of Rights**:
  - **First Amendment**: Freedoms of speech, religion, press, assembly, and petition.
  - **Second Amendment**: Right to bear arms.
  - **Third Amendment**: Protection from quartering soldiers.
  - **Fourth Amendment**: Protection against unreasonable searches and seizures.
  - **Fifth to Eighth Amendments**: Rights related to legal proceedings, including due process, self-incrimination, and protection from cruel and unusual punishment.
  - **Ninth Amendment**: Acknowledgment that other rights exist beyond those listed.
  - **Tenth Amendment**: Powers not delegated to the federal government are reserved to the states or the people.

8.4 The Impact on the Constitution and Future Governance

Shaping the Nation's Foundational Principles
The debates between Federalists and Anti-Federalists had profound effects on the Constitution's final form and the trajectory of American governance.

Establishment of a Strong Yet Limited Government
- **Balanced Power**: The Constitution created a federal government strong enough to function effectively while incorporating mechanisms to prevent tyranny.
- **Federalism**: Defined the division of powers between the national government and the states.

Protection of Individual Liberties
- **Bill of Rights**: The first ten amendments enshrined essential freedoms and legal protections, addressing Anti-Federalist concerns.
- **Ongoing Relevance**: These rights continue to be fundamental in legal interpretations and societal values.

Precedent for Amendment
- **Flexible Framework**: The amendment process demonstrated the Constitution's ability to adapt over time.
- **Encouraging Civic Engagement**: Highlighted the importance of public discourse and participation in shaping government policy.

Formation of Political Parties
- **Federalist Party**:
  - **Leaders**: Alexander Hamilton, John Adams.
  - **Policies**: Favored strong central government, commercial economy, and close ties with Britain.
- **Democratic-Republican Party**:
  - **Leaders**: Thomas Jefferson, James Madison.
  - **Policies**: Advocated for states' rights, agrarian interests, and support for the French Revolution.
- **Significance**: The Federalist and Anti-Federalist factions evolved into the first political parties, influencing the nation's political landscape.

8.5 Legacy of the Debates

Continuing Influence on American Democracy
The dialogues and disagreements of this era have left an enduring mark on the United States.

Emphasis on Rights and Liberties
- **Judicial Interpretation**: The Bill of Rights serves as a cornerstone for Supreme Court decisions on civil liberties.
- **Civil Rights Movements**: Groups have invoked these amendments to advance equality and justice.

Federal-State Relations
- **Ongoing Tension**: Debates over the balance of power continue in issues like education, healthcare, and environmental regulation.
- **Legal Challenges**: States often test the limits of federal authority, reflecting the Anti-Federalist emphasis on local control.

Public Participation
- **Engaged Citizenry**: The ratification debates underscore the importance of informed and active involvement in governance.
- **Democratic Processes**: Encourages vigilance in protecting rights and holding government accountable.

Chapter 9: Introducing the First Ten Amendments

As you continue your exploration of the United States Constitution, this chapter focuses on the first ten amendments, collectively known as the **Bill of Rights**. Ratified in 1791, these amendments were pivotal in addressing concerns about individual liberties and limitations on governmental power. Understanding the origins and content of the Bill of Rights provides crucial insight into the protections that are fundamental to American democracy.

9.1 Protecting Individual Liberties

The Necessity of Enumerated Rights

The inclusion of the Bill of Rights was not originally part of the Constitution drafted at the Constitutional Convention in 1787. The framers debated whether explicit protections were necessary, given that they believed the Constitution's structure already limited governmental overreach. However, the **Anti-Federalists** strongly argued for specific guarantees to safeguard individual freedoms and prevent potential tyranny.

Origins of the Bill of Rights

- **Anti-Federalist Advocacy**:
  - **Fear of Centralized Power**: Anti-Federalists worried that a strong federal government could infringe upon personal liberties, much like the British Crown had done.
  - **Demand for Protections**: They insisted that without explicit rights, citizens would be vulnerable to oppression.
- **Federalist Response**:
  - **Initial Resistance**: Federalists like **James Madison** believed that enumerating rights might limit them, implying that unlisted rights were unprotected.
  - **Pragmatic Shift**: To ensure ratification of the Constitution and unify the nation, Federalists agreed to add amendments safeguarding individual liberties.
- **James Madison's Role**:
  - **Champion of the Bill of Rights**: Though initially skeptical, Madison became a key advocate for the amendments.
  - **Drafting the Amendments**: He reviewed over 200 suggestions from states and distilled them into proposed amendments.

The Ratification Process

- **First Congress (1789)**:
  - **Introduction of Amendments**: Madison presented 19 amendments to Congress.
  - **Congressional Approval**: After debates and revisions, Congress approved 12 amendments to send to the states.
- **State Ratification**:
  - **Adoption**: By December 15, 1791, three-fourths of the states ratified ten of the twelve amendments.
  - **Significance**: The ratified amendments became the Bill of Rights, embedding essential protections into the Constitution.

Importance of the Bill of Rights

- **Limiting Government Power**: Clearly delineated what the federal government could not do, thus protecting citizens' freedoms.
- **Promoting Trust**: Helped alleviate fears of a too-powerful central government, encouraging unity and support for the new Constitution.
- **Foundation for Future Rights**: Established a precedent for amending the Constitution to expand and clarify rights.

9.2 Amendment by Amendment

Detailed Explanations of Each Right Granted

The Bill of Rights encompasses a range of protections that are foundational to American law and society. Let's delve into each amendment to understand the rights and freedoms they guarantee.

First Amendment

"Congress shall make no law respecting an establishment of religion, or prohibiting the free exercise thereof; or abridging the freedom of speech, or of the press; or the right of the people peaceably to assemble, and to petition the Government for a redress of grievances."

Key Protections

1. **Freedom of Religion**:

- **Establishment Clause**: Prohibits the government from establishing an official religion or favoring one religion over others.
- **Free Exercise Clause**: Protects individuals' rights to practice their religion without governmental interference.

2. **Freedom of Speech**:
   - **Expression Rights**: Allows individuals to speak freely, including criticizing the government.
   - **Limitations**: Does not protect speech that incites violence, defames others, or constitutes obscenity.
3. **Freedom of the Press**:
   - **Media Rights**: Ensures that the press can report news and opinions without censorship.
4. **Freedom of Assembly**:
   - **Peaceful Gathering**: Grants the right to hold public meetings and demonstrations.
5. **Right to Petition**:
   - **Government Accountability**: Allows citizens to petition the government to address grievances.

Significance
- **Cornerstone of Democracy**: These freedoms are essential for open discourse, accountability, and the exchange of ideas in a democratic society.

Second Amendment
"A well regulated Militia, being necessary to the security of a free State, the right of the people to keep and bear Arms, shall not be infringed."

Key Protections
- **Right to Bear Arms**:
   - **Individual Right**: Protects the individual's right to possess and carry weapons.
   - **Militia Context**: References the importance of a regulated militia for state security.

Interpretations and Debates
- **Individual vs. Collective Rights**: Ongoing debates center on whether the amendment protects individual gun ownership or is tied to militia service.
- **Regulation**: Discussions about the extent to which the government can regulate firearms.

Significance
- **Personal Security**: Seen by many as a means to protect oneself and resist oppression.
- **Cultural Impact**: Firearms have played a significant role in American history and identity.

Third Amendment
"No Soldier shall, in time of peace be quartered in any house, without the consent of the Owner, nor in time of war, but in a manner to be prescribed by law."

Key Protections
- **Protection from Quartering Troops**:
   - **Consent Requirement**: Soldiers cannot be housed in private residences without the owner's permission.
   - **Legal Process**: Even in wartime, there must be lawful procedures in place.

Historical Context
- **Colonial Grievances**: Reaction to British practices of quartering troops in colonists' homes.

Significance
- **Privacy and Property Rights**: Emphasizes the sanctity of one's home and personal property.

Fourth Amendment
"The right of the people to be secure in their persons, houses, papers, and effects, against unreasonable searches and seizures, shall not be violated, and no Warrants shall issue, but upon probable cause, supported by Oath or affirmation, and particularly describing the place to be searched, and the persons or things to be seized."

Key Protections
- **Protection Against Unreasonable Searches and Seizures**:
   - **Privacy Rights**: Ensures personal privacy and security from arbitrary governmental intrusions.
- **Warrant Requirements**:
   - **Probable Cause**: Warrants must be issued based on credible evidence.

- o **Specificity**: Warrants must clearly define the scope of the search and items sought.

Significance
- **Legal Safeguards**: Establishes fundamental procedures for law enforcement to protect citizens' rights.

Fifth Amendment
"No person shall be held to answer for a capital, or otherwise infamous crime, unless on a presentment or indictment of a Grand Jury... nor shall any person be subject for the same offence to be twice put in jeopardy... nor shall be compelled in any criminal case to be a witness against himself... nor be deprived of life, liberty, or property, without due process of law... nor shall private property be taken for public use, without just compensation."

Key Protections
1. **Grand Jury Indictment**:
   - o **Serious Charges**: Requires a grand jury indictment for capital or infamous crimes.
2. **Double Jeopardy**:
   - o **No Repeated Trials**: Prohibits being tried twice for the same offense.
3. **Self-Incrimination**:
   - o **Right to Remain Silent**: Individuals cannot be compelled to testify against themselves.
4. **Due Process**:
   - o **Fair Treatment**: Guarantees legal proceedings will be fair and follow established rules.
5. **Eminent Domain**:
   - o **Just Compensation**: If private property is taken for public use, the owner must be fairly compensated.

Significance
- **Protection of Legal Rights**: Ensures fairness in the justice system and protects against government abuse.

Sixth Amendment
"In all criminal prosecutions, the accused shall enjoy the right to a speedy and public trial, by an impartial jury... to be informed of the nature and cause of the accusation; to be confronted with the witnesses against him; to have compulsory process for obtaining witnesses in his favor, and to have the Assistance of Counsel for his defence."

Key Protections
1. **Speedy and Public Trial**:
   - o **Timely Justice**: Prevents undue delays in legal proceedings.
2. **Impartial Jury**:
   - o **Fair Judgment**: Ensures the jury is unbiased and representative.
3. **Notification of Charges**:
   - o **Understanding Accusations**: The accused must be informed of the specific charges.
4. **Confrontation Clause**:
   - o **Cross-Examination**: Allows the accused to question witnesses testifying against them.
5. **Compulsory Process**:
   - o **Obtaining Witnesses**: The accused can compel witnesses to testify on their behalf.
6. **Right to Counsel**:
   - o **Legal Representation**: Guarantees the assistance of an attorney.

Significance
- **Fair Trial Rights**: Fundamental to ensuring justice and preventing wrongful convictions.

Seventh Amendment
"In Suits at common law, where the value in controversy shall exceed twenty dollars, the right of trial by jury shall be preserved, and no fact tried by a jury shall be otherwise re-examined in any Court of the United States, than according to the rules of the common law."

Key Protections
- **Civil Trial by Jury**:
  - o **Jury Rights**: Guarantees a jury trial in federal civil cases exceeding a specified amount.
- **Limitation on Re-Examination**:
  - o **Respecting Jury Findings**: Courts must respect the jury's findings of fact.

Significance
- **Preservation of Common Law Traditions**: Upholds historical legal practices and reinforces the role of juries.

Eighth Amendment
"Excessive bail shall not be required, nor excessive fines imposed, nor cruel and unusual punishments inflicted."

Key Protections

1. **Excessive Bail and Fines**:
   - **Financial Fairness**: Prevents the government from imposing unreasonably high bail or fines.
2. **Cruel and Unusual Punishment**:
   - **Humane Treatment**: Prohibits barbaric punishments and ensures penalties are proportionate to the offense.

Significance
- **Human Rights Protection**: Reflects a commitment to dignity and fairness in the justice system.

Ninth Amendment
"The enumeration in the Constitution, of certain rights, shall not be construed to deny or disparage others retained by the people."

Key Protections
- **Unenumerated Rights**:
  - **Acknowledgment of Additional Rights**: Recognizes that citizens possess rights beyond those explicitly listed in the Constitution.
- **Preventing Narrow Interpretation**:
  - **Broad Protection**: Ensures that listing specific rights does not imply the absence of others.

Significance
- **Flexibility and Inclusivity**: Allows for the recognition of fundamental rights as society evolves.

Tenth Amendment
"The powers not delegated to the United States by the Constitution, nor prohibited by it to the States, are reserved to the States respectively, or to the people."

Key Protections
- **Federalism Principle**:
  - **State Sovereignty**: Affirms that powers not granted to the federal government are retained by the states or the people.
- **Limitation of Federal Power**:
  - **Balance of Authority**: Helps define the division of power between federal and state governments.

Significance
- **Protection of States' Rights**: Emphasizes the importance of local control and prevents federal overreach.

Chapter 10: The Impact on American Society

As you continue this exploration of the United States' foundational documents, this chapter examines how the **Constitution** and the **Bill of Rights** have profoundly influenced American society. The principles enshrined in these documents have shaped legal interpretations, social movements, and the nation's collective identity. Understanding their impact provides insight into the ongoing evolution of American democracy and the challenges and triumphs experienced along the way.

10.1 Early Interpretations

How Courts Began to Apply the Bill of Rights

In the years following the ratification of the Constitution and the Bill of Rights, the interpretation and application of these documents began to take shape through judicial decisions and legislative actions.

The Role of the Supreme Court

- **Establishment of Judicial Review**:
  - **Marbury v. Madison (1803)**: This landmark case, presided over by Chief Justice **John Marshall**, established the principle of judicial review, allowing the Supreme Court to declare laws unconstitutional.
  - **Significance**: Empowered the judiciary to interpret the Constitution and ensure that legislative and executive actions comply with its provisions.

Initial Limitations

- **Applicability to Federal Government Only**:
  - **Barron v. Baltimore (1833)**: The Supreme Court ruled that the Bill of Rights restricted only the federal government, not the states.
  - **Impact**: Meant that state governments were not bound by the Bill of Rights, limiting its immediate effect on many citizens' daily lives.

Expansion Through the Fourteenth Amendment

- **Post-Civil War Changes**:
  - **Fourteenth Amendment (1868)**: Introduced the concepts of **due process** and **equal protection** under the law at the state level.
- **Incorporation Doctrine**:
  - **Gradual Application to States**: Through the doctrine of selective incorporation, the Supreme Court began applying Bill of Rights protections to the states.
  - **Key Cases**:
    - **Gitlow v. New York (1925)**: Extended freedom of speech protections to state actions.
    - **Near v. Minnesota (1931)**: Applied freedom of the press to the states.
  - **Significance**: Ensured that individual rights were protected from infringement by both federal and state governments.

10.2 Ongoing Relevance of the Bill of Rights

Modern Cases and Your Rights Today

The Bill of Rights continues to be a living document, with its amendments interpreted and reinterpreted to address contemporary issues.

First Amendment Rights

- **Freedom of Speech and Expression**:
  - **Tinker v. Des Moines (1969)**:
    - **Issue**: Students wearing armbands to protest the Vietnam War.
    - **Ruling**: Protected symbolic speech in schools.
  - **Citizens United v. FEC (2010)**:
    - **Issue**: Corporate spending in elections.
    - **Ruling**: Political spending is a form of protected speech.
- **Freedom of Religion**:
  - **Engel v. Vitale (1962)**:
    - **Issue**: State-sponsored prayer in public schools.
    - **Ruling**: Violated the Establishment Clause.
  - **Burwell v. Hobby Lobby Stores, Inc. (2014)**:
    - **Issue**: Religious objections to contraceptive mandate.
    - **Ruling**: Certain for-profit corporations can be exempt based on religious beliefs.

Second Amendment Rights
- **Right to Bear Arms**:
  - **District of Columbia v. Heller (2008)**:
    - **Issue**: Washington D.C.'s handgun ban.
    - **Ruling**: Affirmed an individual's right to possess firearms unconnected with service in a militia.
  - **McDonald v. City of Chicago (2010)**:
    - **Issue**: Applicability to states.
    - **Ruling**: Incorporated the Second Amendment to the states through the Fourteenth Amendment.

Fourth Amendment Protections
- **Search and Seizure**:
  - **Mapp v. Ohio (1961)**:
    - **Issue**: Illegally obtained evidence.
    - **Ruling**: Established the exclusionary rule at the state level.
  - **Riley v. California (2014)**:
    - **Issue**: Warrantless search of cell phones.
    - **Ruling**: Police must obtain a warrant to search digital information on a cell phone seized from an individual during an arrest.

Rights of the Accused
- **Fifth and Sixth Amendments**:
  - **Miranda v. Arizona (1966)**:
    - **Issue**: Rights during police interrogations.
    - **Ruling**: Established the requirement for Miranda warnings about the right to remain silent and to an attorney.
  - **Gideon v. Wainwright (1963)**:
    - **Issue**: Right to counsel.
    - **Ruling**: Guaranteed the right to legal representation for criminal defendants in state courts.

Eighth Amendment Issues
- **Cruel and Unusual Punishment**:
  - **Furman v. Georgia (1972)**:
    - **Issue**: Death penalty application.
    - **Ruling**: Led to a temporary halt of capital punishment due to arbitrary sentencing.
  - **Roper v. Simmons (2005)**:
    - **Issue**: Death penalty for minors.
    - **Ruling**: Unconstitutional to impose capital punishment for crimes committed under the age of 18.

Privacy and Personal Autonomy
- **Implied Rights**:
  - **Griswold v. Connecticut (1965)**:
    - **Issue**: State ban on contraceptives.
    - **Ruling**: Recognized a right to privacy within marriage.
  - **Roe v. Wade (1973)**:
    - **Issue**: Abortion rights.
    - **Ruling**: Extended the right to privacy to a woman's decision to have an abortion.
  - **Recent Developments**:
    - **Dobbs v. Jackson Women's Health Organization (2022)**:
      - **Issue**: Overturning Roe v. Wade.
      - **Ruling**: Held that the Constitution does not confer a right to abortion, returning the authority to regulate abortion to the states.

Equal Protection and Civil Rights
- **Fourteenth Amendment Applications**:
  - **Brown v. Board of Education (1954)**:
    - **Issue**: Segregation in public schools.
    - **Ruling**: Declared segregation unconstitutional, overturning "separate but equal."
  - **Obergefell v. Hodges (2015)**:
    - **Issue**: Same-sex marriage.

- **Ruling**: Guaranteed the right to marry for same-sex couples under the Equal Protection Clause.

10.3 Shaping American Legal and Social Thought

The Bill of Rights' Influence on Society

The Constitution and the Bill of Rights have not only guided legal interpretations but have also been instrumental in shaping American culture, politics, and social movements.

Civil Liberties and Social Change

- **Abolitionist Movement**:
  - **Arguments for Freedom**: Advocated that slavery violated the fundamental rights of life and liberty.
- **Women's Suffrage**:
  - **Nineteenth Amendment (1920)**: Granted women the right to vote, expanding democratic principles.
- **Civil Rights Movement**:
  - **Utilizing Constitutional Principles**: Leaders like **Dr. Martin Luther King Jr.** invoked the Constitution to demand equal rights and justice.
  - **Legislation**: Civil Rights Act (1964) and Voting Rights Act (1965) reinforced constitutional protections.

Expansion of Democratic Participation

- **Voting Rights**:
  - **Fifteenth Amendment (1870)**: Prohibited voting restrictions based on race.
  - **Twenty-Sixth Amendment (1971)**: Lowered the voting age to 18.
- **Direct Election of Senators**:
  - **Seventeenth Amendment (1913)**: Established the direct election of senators by the people, enhancing democratic representation.

Cultural and Educational Impact

- **Civic Education**:
  - **Curriculum Integration**: The Constitution and Bill of Rights are integral parts of American education, fostering an informed citizenry.
- **National Identity**:
  - **Shared Values**: These documents promote ideals of freedom, equality, and justice, uniting diverse populations under common principles.

10.4 The Constitution's Role Today

Living Document and Ongoing Debates

The Constitution continues to be a living document, adapting to new circumstances and challenges through interpretation, amendments, and societal engagement.

Modern Constitutional Issues

- **Technology and Privacy**:
  - **Digital Rights**: Questions about data privacy, surveillance, and freedom of expression in the digital age.
- **Second Amendment Debates**:
  - **Gun Control**: Balancing the right to bear arms with concerns about public safety and mass shootings.
- **Freedom of Speech**:
  - **Hate Speech and Social Media**: Addressing the limits of free speech in an interconnected world.

Judicial Philosophy

- **Originalism vs. Living Constitution**:
  - **Originalism**: Interpreting the Constitution based on the framers' original intent.
  - **Living Constitution**: Viewing the Constitution as a dynamic document that evolves with societal changes.
- **Impact on Rulings**:
  - **Judicial Appointments**: Judges' philosophies influence decisions on critical issues.

Amendments and Proposals

- **Constitutional Amendments**:
  - **Rare but Significant**: Amendments address fundamental changes, such as abolishing slavery (Thirteenth Amendment) or establishing income tax (Sixteenth Amendment).
- **Proposed Amendments**:
  - **Equal Rights Amendment**: Aimed to guarantee equal legal rights regardless of sex; not ratified.
  - **Debates Continue**: Proposals reflect ongoing efforts to refine and improve governance.

10.5 Global Influence

How Other Countries Have Drawn Inspiration from the U.S. Constitution

The United States Constitution has served as a model for nations worldwide seeking to establish democratic governance and protect individual rights.

Adoption of Constitutional Principles
- **Separation of Powers**:
  - **Checks and Balances**: Many countries have adopted systems that divide governmental power to prevent tyranny.
- **Bill of Rights Equivalents**:
  - **Rights Protections**: Constitutions around the world include provisions similar to the U.S. Bill of Rights, safeguarding freedoms.

Influence on International Law
- **Universal Declaration of Human Rights (1948)**:
  - **Shared Values**: Reflects principles of liberty and equality promoted by the U.S. Constitution.
- **Democratic Movements**:
  - **Inspiration for Change**: The U.S. constitutional model has inspired reformers and revolutionaries seeking democratic governance.

Challenges and Adaptations
- **Cultural Contexts**:
  - **Customization**: Countries adapt constitutional principles to fit their unique historical and cultural circumstances.
- **Evolution of Governance**:
  - **Continuous Development**: Nations evolve their constitutions to address contemporary issues, much like the U.S. has done.

Chapter 11: Significant Amendments Beyond the Bill of Rights

As you continue your journey through the evolution of the United States Constitution, this chapter focuses on the significant amendments that have shaped the nation's legal and social landscape beyond the original Bill of Rights. These amendments reflect the dynamic nature of the Constitution, addressing pressing issues of their times and expanding the principles of freedom, equality, and justice. Understanding these amendments provides insight into how the Constitution adapts to new challenges and societal changes, reinforcing its role as a living document.

11.1 Civil War Amendments

Abolishing Slavery and Defining Citizenship

The **Thirteenth**, **Fourteenth**, and **Fifteenth Amendments**, collectively known as the **Civil War Amendments**, were ratified in the aftermath of the Civil War (1861–1865). These amendments fundamentally transformed the Constitution by abolishing slavery, defining citizenship, and protecting voting rights, laying the groundwork for future civil rights advancements.

Thirteenth Amendment (1865)

Section 1:
"Neither slavery nor involuntary servitude, except as a punishment for crime whereof the party shall have been duly convicted, shall exist within the United States, or any place subject to their jurisdiction."

Section 2:
"Congress shall have power to enforce this article by appropriate legislation."

Key Provisions
- **Abolition of Slavery**: Officially ended slavery in all states and territories.
- **Involuntary Servitude**: Prohibited forced labor, except as punishment for a crime.
- **Enforcement Power**: Granted Congress the authority to pass laws implementing the amendment.

Historical Context
- **Emancipation Proclamation**: Issued by President Abraham Lincoln in 1863, it declared freedom for enslaved people in Confederate states but did not abolish slavery nationwide.
- **Need for Constitutional Amendment**: Ensured the permanent abolition of slavery beyond wartime measures.

Impact and Significance
- **Legal Foundation for Freedom**: Established a constitutional guarantee against slavery.
- **Challenges**: Despite its passage, practices like sharecropping and Black Codes sought to restrict the freedoms of formerly enslaved individuals.
- **Modern Interpretations**: Invoked in cases addressing forced labor and human trafficking.

Fourteenth Amendment (1868)

Section 1:
"All persons born or naturalized in the United States, and subject to the jurisdiction thereof, are citizens of the United States and of the State wherein they reside. No State shall make or enforce any law which shall abridge the privileges or immunities of citizens... nor shall any State deprive any person of life, liberty, or property, without due process of law; nor deny to any person within its jurisdiction the equal protection of the laws."

Key Provisions
1. **Citizenship Clause**:
   - **Birthright Citizenship**: Grants citizenship to all persons born or naturalized in the U.S.
2. **Privileges or Immunities Clause**:
   - **Protection of Rights**: Prevents states from infringing on citizens' rights.
3. **Due Process Clause**:
   - **Legal Fairness**: States cannot deprive individuals of life, liberty, or property without proper legal procedures.
4. **Equal Protection Clause**:
   - **Equality Under the Law**: Requires states to provide equal legal protections to all people.

Historical Context
- **Reconstruction Era**: Aimed to integrate formerly enslaved people into society as full citizens.
- **Addressing Dred Scott Decision**: Overturned the Supreme Court's ruling that African Americans could not be citizens.

Impact and Significance
- **Foundation for Civil Rights**: Central to landmark cases like **Brown v. Board of**

Education (1954), ending racial segregation in schools.
- **Incorporation Doctrine**: Used to apply Bill of Rights protections to the states.
- **Broad Applications**: Influences cases on privacy, marriage equality, and gender discrimination.

Fifteenth Amendment (1870)
Section 1:
"The right of citizens of the United States to vote shall not be denied or abridged... on account of race, color, or previous condition of servitude."
Section 2:
"Congress shall have power to enforce this article by appropriate legislation."

Key Provisions
- **Voting Rights Protection**: Prohibits denying the right to vote based on race, color, or former enslavement.
- **Enforcement Authority**: Empowers Congress to enact legislation ensuring voting rights.

Historical Context
- **Post-Civil War Adjustments**: Sought to secure political participation for African American men.
- **Resistance and Evasion**: Despite the amendment, discriminatory practices like literacy tests, poll taxes, and intimidation persisted.

Impact and Significance
- **Advancement of Democracy**: Expanded the electorate and promoted political equality.
- **Civil Rights Movement**: The **Voting Rights Act of 1965** strengthened enforcement of the Fifteenth Amendment.
- **Ongoing Challenges**: Contemporary debates over voter ID laws and disenfranchisement reflect the amendment's relevance.

11.2 Progressive Era Changes
Income Tax, Direct Election of Senators, Prohibition, and Women's Suffrage
The late 19th and early 20th centuries, known as the **Progressive Era**, were marked by social and political reforms addressing industrialization's challenges, economic inequality, and calls for greater democratic participation.

Sixteenth Amendment (1913)
Text:
"The Congress shall have power to lay and collect taxes on incomes, from whatever source derived, without apportionment among the several States..."

Key Provisions
- **Federal Income Tax Authority**: Grants Congress the power to levy taxes on individual and corporate incomes.
- **Elimination of Apportionment**: Removes the requirement to distribute taxes based on state populations.

Historical Context
- **Revenue Needs**: Addressed funding for government programs and reducing reliance on tariffs.
- **Supreme Court Rulings**: Overcame previous decisions that limited federal taxation powers.

Impact and Significance
- **Fiscal Policy Tool**: Enabled progressive taxation to address economic disparities.
- **Expansion of Government Services**: Funded public infrastructure, defense, and social programs.
- **Debates on Taxation**: Continues to influence discussions on tax policy and economic equity.

Seventeenth Amendment (1913)
Text:
"The Senate of the United States shall be composed of two Senators from each State, elected by the people thereof..."

Key Provisions
- **Direct Election of Senators**: Transferred the election of senators from state legislatures to the general electorate.
- **Term Details**: Senators serve six-year terms with one vote each.

Historical Context
- **Corruption Concerns**: Addressed issues of bribery and undue influence in state legislatures.
- **Democratic Expansion**: Part of broader efforts to make government more responsive to the people.

Impact and Significance
- **Increased Accountability**: Senators are directly answerable to voters.
- **State-Federal Balance**: Shifted some power from states to the federal government.
- **Voter Engagement**: Encouraged greater public participation in federal elections.

Eighteenth Amendment (1919)
Text:
"...the manufacture, sale, or transportation of intoxicating liquors... for beverage purposes is hereby prohibited."
Key Provisions
- **Prohibition of Alcohol**: Banned the production, sale, and transport of alcoholic beverages.
- **Enforcement Period**: Allowed one year after ratification for implementation.

Historical Context
- **Temperance Movement**: Driven by social reformers aiming to reduce alcohol-related problems.
- **World War I Influence**: Wartime grain conservation and anti-German sentiment bolstered support.

Impact and Significance
- **Rise of Illegal Activities**: Led to bootlegging, speakeasies, and organized crime.
- **Enforcement Challenges**: Difficulties in policing and widespread noncompliance.
- **Repeal**: The **Twenty-First Amendment (1933)** repealed Prohibition, acknowledging its ineffectiveness.

Nineteenth Amendment (1920)
Text:
"The right of citizens of the United States to vote shall not be denied... on account of sex."
Key Provisions
- **Women's Suffrage**: Granted women the right to vote nationwide.
- **Enforcement Clause**: Congress can enact legislation to uphold the amendment.

Historical Context
- **Suffrage Movement**: Decades-long activism by women like Susan B. Anthony and Elizabeth Cady Stanton.
- **World War I Contributions**: Women's roles in the war effort highlighted the need for equal political rights.

Impact and Significance
- **Democratic Expansion**: Doubled the electorate, promoting gender equality in politics.
- **Social Progress**: Paved the way for further advancements in women's rights.
- **Continuing Influence**: Encourages ongoing efforts toward gender equality in various spheres.

11.3 Modern Amendments
From Repealing Prohibition to Presidential Term Limits
The Constitution continued to evolve throughout the 20th century, addressing contemporary issues and refining governmental structures.

Twenty-First Amendment (1933)
Text:
"The eighteenth article of amendment to the Constitution... is hereby repealed."
Key Provisions
- **Repeal of Prohibition**: Ended the nationwide ban on alcohol established by the Eighteenth Amendment.
- **State Control**: Granted states the authority to regulate alcohol within their borders.

Historical Context
- **Great Depression**: Economic hardships increased the desire for legal alcohol sales and associated tax revenues.
- **Public Opinion Shift**: Recognition that Prohibition was unenforceable and had unintended negative consequences.

Impact and Significance
- **Regulatory Framework**: States established their own laws regarding alcohol.
- **Economic Benefits**: Boosted industries and provided government revenue.
- **Policy Lessons**: Highlighted the complexities of legislating personal behavior.

Twenty-Second Amendment (1951)
Text:
"No person shall be elected to the office of the President more than twice..."
Key Provisions
- **Presidential Term Limits**: Limits individuals to two elected terms as President.
- **Applicability**: Addresses those who assume the presidency through succession.

Historical Context
- **Franklin D. Roosevelt's Four Terms**: Prompted concerns over prolonged executive power.
- **Tradition of Two Terms**: Following George Washington's precedent, respected until FDR.

Impact and Significance

- **Executive Power Check**: Prevents potential for authoritarianism through extended tenure.
- **Political Dynamics**: Influences succession planning and party strategies.
- **Debate Over Limits**: Ongoing discussions about the benefits and drawbacks of term restrictions.

Twenty-Fourth Amendment (1964)

Text:
"The right of citizens... to vote... shall not be denied... by reason of failure to pay any poll tax or other tax."

Key Provisions
- **Abolition of Poll Taxes**: Prohibits the use of poll taxes in federal elections.
- **Enforcement Clause**: Empowers Congress to enforce the amendment through legislation.

Historical Context
- **Voting Barriers**: Poll taxes were used primarily in Southern states to disenfranchise African American voters and poor whites.
- **Civil Rights Movement**: Efforts to eliminate discriminatory practices in voting.

Impact and Significance
- **Expansion of Voting Rights**: Removed economic barriers to participation in federal elections.
- **Foundation for Further Reforms**: Supported subsequent legislation like the **Voting Rights Act of 1965**.
- **State Elections**: Supreme Court later ruled poll taxes unconstitutional in state elections as well.

Twenty-Sixth Amendment (1971)

Text:
"The right of citizens... who are eighteen years of age or older, to vote shall not be denied... on account of age."

Key Provisions
- **Lowering Voting Age**: Extended the right to vote to citizens aged 18 and older.
- **Enforcement Clause**: Allows Congress to enact legislation to uphold the amendment.

Historical Context
- **Vietnam War Era**: "Old enough to fight, old enough to vote" became a rallying cry, highlighting the inconsistency of drafting 18-year-olds who lacked voting rights.
- **Youth Activism**: Increased political engagement among young people.

Impact and Significance
- **Democratic Inclusion**: Expanded the electorate, recognizing the maturity and responsibilities of younger citizens.
- **Political Engagement**: Encouraged youth participation in politics and policy-making.
- **Ongoing Challenges**: Voter turnout among young adults remains a focus of civic initiatives.

11.4 Process and Debates

How Amendments Get Proposed, Ratified, and Interpreted

The process of amending the Constitution is deliberately rigorous, ensuring that changes reflect a broad consensus. Understanding this process highlights the balance between flexibility and stability in constitutional governance.

Amendment Proposal Methods
1. **Congressional Proposal**:
   - **Two-Thirds Vote**: Requires approval from two-thirds of both the House of Representatives and the Senate.
2. **Constitutional Convention**:
   - **State Legislatures**: Two-thirds (currently 34) of state legislatures can call for a convention to propose amendments.

Ratification Methods
1. **State Legislatures**:
   - **Three-Fourths Approval**: Amendments must be ratified by three-fourths (currently 38) of state legislatures.
2. **State Conventions**:
   - **Special Conventions**: Used only once, for the Twenty-First Amendment, allowing for a more direct expression of the people's will.

Chapter 12: The Amendment Process

As you delve deeper into the Constitution, it's important to understand that this foundational document was designed not as a static set of rules but as a living framework capable of evolving with the nation. The **Amendment Process** outlined in the Constitution provides a structured method for making changes, ensuring that the document can adapt to new circumstances while maintaining its core principles. In this chapter, we'll explore how amendments are proposed and ratified, and we'll examine some notable proposed amendments that didn't make it into the Constitution, shedding light on the dynamic nature of American governance.

12.1 How Amendments Are Made

Proposal and Ratification Steps

The framers of the Constitution recognized that future generations might need to make alterations or additions to the document. To facilitate this, they included **Article V**, which outlines the process for amending the Constitution. This process is deliberately rigorous, requiring broad consensus to ensure that changes reflect the will of a significant portion of the populace.

Article V of the Constitution

Text:

"The Congress, whenever two thirds of both Houses shall deem it necessary, shall propose Amendments to this Constitution, or, on the Application of the Legislatures of two thirds of the several States, shall call a Convention for proposing Amendments, which, in either Case, shall be valid to all Intents and Purposes, as part of this Constitution, when ratified by the Legislatures of three fourths of the several States or by Conventions in three fourths thereof..."

Two Methods of Proposing Amendments

1. **Congressional Proposal**
   - **Initiation:** An amendment can be proposed by a two-thirds majority vote in both the House of Representatives and the Senate.
   - **Usage:** This is the most common method; all 27 ratified amendments have been proposed this way.
   - **Process:**
     - **Drafting:** An amendment is introduced as a joint resolution in Congress.
     - **Debate and Vote:** It must pass both chambers by a two-thirds majority.
     - **Transmission to States:** The proposed amendment is sent to the states for ratification.

2. **Constitutional Convention**
   - **Initiation:** An amendment can be proposed by a convention called for by two-thirds (currently 34) of the state legislatures.
   - **Usage:** This method has never been used to successfully propose an amendment.
   - **Process:**
     - **Application by States:** State legislatures apply to Congress to call a convention.
     - **Convention Proceedings:** Delegates propose amendments.
     - **Transmission to States:** Any proposed amendments are sent to the states for ratification.

Two Methods of Ratification

Once an amendment is proposed, it must be ratified by the states through one of two methods:

1. **State Legislatures**
   - **Requirement:** Approval by three-fourths (currently 38) of the state legislatures.
   - **Process:**
     - **Consideration:** Each state's legislature debates and votes on the amendment.
     - **Approval:** A simple majority is typically required in each legislature.

2. **State Conventions**
   - **Requirement:** Approval by conventions in three-fourths of the states.
   - **Usage:** Only the Twenty-First Amendment (repealing Prohibition) was ratified this way.
   - **Process:**

- **Convention Call:** States convene special ratifying conventions.
- **Delegate Selection:** Delegates are chosen, often by popular vote.
- **Debate and Vote:** Delegates debate the amendment and vote.

Time Frame for Ratification
- **Congressional Discretion:** Congress may set a deadline for ratification, typically seven years.
- **Extensions:** Deadlines can be extended by Congress, as seen with the Equal Rights Amendment, although this is subject to legal debate.
- **No Deadline:** Some amendments, like the Twenty-Seventh Amendment (dealing with congressional pay), had no deadline and were ratified many years after proposal.

Examples of Successful Amendments
- **Bill of Rights (1791):** The first ten amendments were ratified to guarantee individual liberties.
- **Civil War Amendments (1865–1870):** Thirteenth, Fourteenth, and Fifteenth Amendments abolished slavery and established citizenship and voting rights.
- **Progressive Era Amendments (1913–1920):** Sixteenth through Nineteenth Amendments addressed income tax, direct election of senators, Prohibition, and women's suffrage.

The Rigorous Nature of the Process
- **Deliberate Difficulty:** The two-thirds and three-fourths requirements ensure that only amendments with widespread support become part of the Constitution.
- **Protection Against Hasty Changes:** The stringent process guards against impulsive or reactionary amendments that may not stand the test of time.

12.2 Notable Proposed Amendments

What Didn't Make It into the Constitution

Throughout American history, numerous amendments have been proposed but failed to be ratified. Examining these unsuccessful attempts offers insight into the political climate of different eras and the evolving priorities of the nation.

The Equal Rights Amendment (ERA)
- **Text:** *"Equality of rights under the law shall not be denied or abridged by the United States or by any State on account of sex."*
- **History:**
  - **First Introduced:** In 1923 by suffragist Alice Paul.
  - **Congressional Approval:** Passed by Congress in 1972 with a seven-year ratification deadline.
  - **Ratification Efforts:**
    - **Initial Support:** Quickly ratified by 35 states.
    - **Opposition:** Faced backlash over concerns about gender roles and the potential impact on laws related to marriage, the draft, and privacy.
    - **Deadline Extension:** Extended to 1982, but no additional states ratified.
  - **Recent Developments:**
    - **Renewed Interest:** In the 2010s, three more states ratified the ERA, reaching the required 38.
    - **Legal Challenges:** Questions remain about the validity of late ratifications and the expired deadline.
- **Significance:**
  - **Women's Rights Movement:** Symbolizes the ongoing struggle for gender equality.
  - **Legal Impact:** Despite not being ratified, it has influenced legislation and court decisions.

The District of Columbia Voting Rights Amendment
- **Purpose:** Intended to grant the District of Columbia full representation in Congress, participation in the Electoral College, and a role in amending the Constitution.
- **History:**
  - **Congressional Approval:** Passed by Congress in 1978.
  - **Ratification Period:** Given seven years for ratification.
  - **Outcome:** Only 16 states ratified before the deadline.

- **Significance:**
  - **Representation Issues:** Highlights the ongoing debate over the political rights of D.C. residents.
  - **Current Status:** Discussions continue about D.C. statehood or alternative methods to provide representation.

The Child Labor Amendment
- **Purpose:** Aimed to grant Congress the authority to regulate labor of persons under 18 years of age.
- **History:**
  - **Congressional Approval:** Passed in 1924.
  - **Ratification Efforts:** Only 28 states have ratified; no deadline was set.
- **Significance:**
  - **Legal Context:** The Supreme Court had previously struck down federal child labor laws.
  - **Resolution:** Later, the Fair Labor Standards Act of 1938 effectively addressed child labor without the amendment.

The Titles of Nobility Amendment
- **Text:** Proposed to revoke the citizenship of any U.S. citizen who accepts a title of nobility from a foreign government.
- **History:**
  - **Congressional Approval:** Passed in 1810.
  - **Ratification Efforts:** Ratified by 12 states, short of the required number at the time.
- **Significance:**
  - **Historical Context:** Reflects early American concerns about foreign influence and maintaining a republican form of government.
  - **Modern Relevance:** Occasionally resurfaces in discussions about citizenship and allegiance.

Balanced Budget Amendment
- **Purpose:** Would require the federal government to not spend more than its income.
- **History:**
  - **Congressional Attempts:** Numerous proposals have been introduced since the 1930s.
  - **Closest Vote:** In 1995, it passed the House but fell one vote short in the Senate.
- **Arguments For:**
  - **Fiscal Responsibility:** Advocates argue it would control national debt and government spending.
- **Arguments Against:**
  - **Economic Flexibility:** Opponents contend it would hinder the government's ability to respond to economic crises.
- **Significance:**
  - **Ongoing Debate:** Reflects concerns over fiscal policy and national debt.

Flag Desecration Amendment
- **Purpose:** Seeks to empower Congress to prohibit the physical desecration of the U.S. flag.
- **History:**
  - **Supreme Court Rulings:** In **Texas v. Johnson** (1989) and **United States v. Eichman** (1990), flag burning was deemed protected speech under the First Amendment.
  - **Congressional Attempts:** Multiple proposals have passed the House but failed to secure the necessary votes in the Senate.
- **Significance:**
  - **Free Speech vs. Patriotism:** Balances constitutional protections of expression with symbols of national identity.
  - **Public Opinion:** Divided views on whether flag desecration should be prohibited.

12.3 The Living Constitution

The Amendment Process as a Reflection of Societal Change

The Constitution's ability to be amended is a testament to its enduring flexibility. The amendment process allows the nation to address new challenges, reinterpret values, and strive toward a more inclusive and just society.

Adaptation Over Time
- **Social Progress:** Amendments have often been catalysts for social change, such as abolishing slavery and extending voting rights.
- **Technological Advances:** Future amendments may address issues like digital privacy or bioethics.

Challenges in Amending
- **High Thresholds:** The rigorous requirements ensure stability but can make necessary changes difficult.
- **Political Polarization:** Consensus is harder to achieve in a divided political climate.

Alternative Methods of Constitutional Change
- **Judicial Interpretation:** Courts, especially the Supreme Court, play a significant role in interpreting the Constitution's meaning.
- **Legislation:** Congress can pass laws that address issues without formal amendments, though these can be challenged in courts.
- **Informal Practices:** Traditions and norms, such as the two-term limit for presidents before the Twenty-Second Amendment, influence governance.

The Role of Citizens
- **Civic Engagement:** Public awareness and activism are crucial in initiating and supporting amendments.
- **Education:** Understanding the Constitution empowers citizens to participate effectively in democracy.

Chapter 13: The Role of the Supreme Court

The **Supreme Court of the United States** stands as one of the most influential institutions in American governance. As the highest judicial authority, it serves as the ultimate arbiter of constitutional interpretation, shaping the nation's laws and, by extension, its society. This chapter explores the establishment of the Supreme Court, its powers and functions, landmark cases that have defined its role, and its profound impact on American life.

13.1 Establishment and Constitutional Basis

Origins and Constitutional Foundations

The Supreme Court was established by the **Constitution** as part of the federal judiciary, designed to interpret laws and ensure justice under the Constitution.

Article III of the Constitution
- **Section 1: Judicial Power**
  - **Creation of the Supreme Court**: The Constitution establishes "one supreme Court" and allows Congress to create inferior courts.
  - **Lifetime Tenure**: Judges hold their offices during good behavior, ensuring judicial independence.
  - **Compensation**: Judges receive a salary that cannot be diminished during their continuance in office.
- **Section 2: Jurisdiction**
  - **Scope of Judicial Power**: Extends to all cases arising under the Constitution, federal laws, and treaties.
  - **Original Jurisdiction**: Cases involving ambassadors, public ministers, consuls, and those in which a state is a party.
  - **Appellate Jurisdiction**: The Court hears appeals from lower federal and state courts.

Judiciary Act of 1789
- **Establishment of Federal Judiciary**: Congress passed this act to set up the federal court system, including the Supreme Court.
- **Number of Justices**: Initially set at six, the number has changed over time and currently stands at nine.
- **Creation of Lower Courts**: Established district courts and circuit courts to handle federal cases.

First Supreme Court
- **First Chief Justice**: **John Jay** served from 1789 to 1795.
- **Early Challenges**: The Court initially had limited power and prestige, with few significant cases in its early years.

13.2 Judicial Review and Marbury v. Madison

Establishing the Power to Interpret the Constitution

One of the most critical developments in the Supreme Court's history was the establishment of **judicial review**, the power to declare laws unconstitutional.

Marbury v. Madison (1803)
- **Background**:
  - **Midnight Appointments**: In the final days of President John Adams' administration, he appointed several justices of the peace, including **William Marbury**.
  - **Withheld Commissions**: Incoming Secretary of State **James Madison** refused to deliver the commissions.
  - **Marbury's Lawsuit**: Marbury petitioned the Supreme Court for a writ of mandamus to compel delivery.
- **Chief Justice John Marshall**:
  - **Leadership**: Served as Chief Justice from 1801 to 1835, significantly shaping the Court's role.
  - **Decision**:
    - **Jurisdiction Issue**: Ruled that the Court did not have original jurisdiction to issue a writ of mandamus in this case.
    - **Judiciary Act Conflict**: Found that the provision of the Judiciary Act of 1789 granting the Court this power was unconstitutional.
    - **Establishment of Judicial Review**: Asserted the Court's authority to review and

nullify congressional acts that conflict with the Constitution.
- **Significance**:
  - **Balance of Powers**: Reinforced the judiciary as an equal branch of government.
  - **Constitutional Interpretation**: Positioned the Supreme Court as the final interpreter of constitutional meaning.

13.3 Landmark Cases Shaping Constitutional Law

Influential Decisions and Their Impact

The Supreme Court has ruled on numerous cases that have profoundly affected American law and society. These landmark decisions illustrate the Court's role in interpreting the Constitution and shaping public policy.

McCulloch v. Maryland (1819)

- **Issue**: Whether Congress had the authority to establish a national bank and if a state could tax it.
- **Decision**:
  - **Implied Powers**: Affirmed Congress's implied powers under the **Necessary and Proper Clause**.
  - **Federal Supremacy**: Established that states cannot tax federal institutions, reinforcing the **Supremacy Clause**.
- **Impact**:
  - **Strengthened Federal Power**: Expanded the scope of federal legislative authority.

Gibbons v. Ogden (1824)

- **Issue**: Regulation of interstate commerce and conflicting steamboat operation licenses.
- **Decision**:
  - **Commerce Clause**: Asserted federal control over interstate commerce.
- **Impact**:
  - **Federal Economic Authority**: Laid the groundwork for federal regulation of economic activities.

Dred Scott v. Sandford (1857)

- **Issue**: Enslaved man Dred Scott sued for his freedom based on residence in free territories.
- **Decision**:
  - **Citizenship Denied**: Ruled that African Americans were not citizens and had no standing to sue.
  - **Missouri Compromise Unconstitutional**: Declared that Congress lacked authority to prohibit slavery in territories.
- **Impact**:
  - **Increased Tensions**: Deepened national divisions leading to the Civil War.
  - **Overturned by the Fourteenth Amendment**: Established birthright citizenship.

Plessy v. Ferguson (1896)

- **Issue**: Constitutionality of racial segregation laws under the "separate but equal" doctrine.
- **Decision**:
  - **Segregation Upheld**: Ruled that separate facilities for races were constitutional if equal.
- **Impact**:
  - **Institutionalized Segregation**: Legitimized Jim Crow laws, leading to widespread discrimination.
  - **Overturned by Brown v. Board of Education**.

Brown v. Board of Education (1954)

- **Issue**: Segregation in public schools challenged as violating the Equal Protection Clause.
- **Decision**:
  - **Segregation Unconstitutional**: Declared that "separate educational facilities are inherently unequal."
- **Impact**:
  - **Civil Rights Movement Catalyst**: Spurred efforts to end racial segregation and discrimination.

Miranda v. Arizona (1966)

- **Issue**: Rights of suspects during police interrogations.
- **Decision**:
  - **Miranda Rights**: Established that suspects must be informed of their rights to remain silent and to an attorney.
- **Impact**:

- o **Due Process Protections**: Enhanced the rights of the accused under the Fifth and Sixth Amendments.

Roe v. Wade (1973)
- **Issue**: Constitutionality of state laws restricting abortion.
- **Decision**:
  - o **Right to Privacy**: Recognized a woman's right to choose abortion under the Fourteenth Amendment.
- **Impact**:
  - o **Reproductive Rights Debate**: Central to ongoing discussions about abortion laws.
  - o **Recent Developments**: Dobbs v. Jackson Women's Health Organization (2022) overturned Roe, returning the regulation of abortion to the states.

United States v. Nixon (1974)
- **Issue**: Presidential privilege and the demand for tapes related to the Watergate scandal.
- **Decision**:
  - o **Limited Executive Privilege**: Ruled that the President is not above the law and must comply with judicial subpoenas.
- **Impact**:
  - o **Rule of Law Affirmed**: Reinforced the principle that no one, not even the President, is above the law.

Obergefell v. Hodges (2015)
- **Issue**: Same-sex couples seeking the right to marry.
- **Decision**:
  - o **Marriage Equality**: Held that the Fourteenth Amendment requires states to license and recognize same-sex marriages.
- **Impact**:
  - o **Expansion of Civil Rights**: Significant victory for LGBTQ+ rights.

13.4 The Supreme Court's Influence on American Society

Balancing Rights, Liberties, and Government Powers

The Supreme Court plays a critical role in interpreting the Constitution and balancing individual rights with governmental interests.

Protector of Individual Rights
- **First Amendment Freedoms**:
  - o **Freedom of Speech and Press**: Cases like **New York Times Co. v. United States (1971)** upheld press freedom against prior restraint.
  - o **Symbolic Speech**: **Texas v. Johnson (1989)** protected flag burning as free speech.
- **Due Process and Equal Protection**:
  - o **Gideon v. Wainwright (1963)**: Guaranteed the right to counsel for criminal defendants.
  - o **Loving v. Virginia (1967)**: Struck down bans on interracial marriage.

Interpreter of Federal and State Powers
- **Federalism**:
  - o **National Federation of Independent Business v. Sebelius (2012)**: Addressed the limits of federal power under the Commerce Clause and taxing authority.
- **State Sovereignty**:
  - o **Printz v. United States (1997)**: Limited federal government's ability to compel state officials to enforce federal law.

Arbiter of Social and Moral Issues
- **Privacy Rights**:
  - o **Griswold v. Connecticut (1965)**: Recognized privacy in marital relations.
  - o **Lawrence v. Texas (2003)**: Struck down laws criminalizing same-sex intimacy.
- **Death Penalty and Criminal Justice**:
  - o **Furman v. Georgia (1972)**: Temporarily halted capital punishment due to arbitrary sentencing.
  - o **Gregg v. Georgia (1976)**: Reinstated the death penalty under revised statutes.

Economic Regulation and Business
- **Antitrust Laws**:
  - o **Standard Oil Co. of New Jersey v. United States (1911)**: Broke up monopolies under antitrust laws.
- **Labor Rights**:

- National Labor Relations Board v. Jones & Laughlin Steel Corp. (1937): Upheld federal regulation of labor relations.

13.5 The Supreme Court's Functioning and Composition

Appointment Process and Court Dynamics
Understanding how the Supreme Court operates and how justices are selected provides insight into its role and influence.

Appointment of Justices
- **Nomination**:
  - **Presidential Selection**: The President nominates candidates for the Supreme Court.
  - **Criteria**: Legal expertise, judicial philosophy, political considerations, and diversity.
- **Confirmation**:
  - **Senate Judiciary Committee**: Holds hearings to question the nominee.
  - **Senate Vote**: Confirmation requires a majority vote in the Senate.
- **Lifetime Tenure**:
  - **Judicial Independence**: Lifetime appointments insulate justices from political pressures.

Composition of the Court
- **Number of Justices**:
  - **Set by Congress**: Currently nine justices, including one Chief Justice and eight Associate Justices.
- **Court's Ideological Balance**:
  - **Shifts Over Time**: The Court's decisions can reflect the prevailing judicial philosophies of its members.
  - **Impact of Appointments**: Presidential nominations can influence the Court's direction for decades.

Decision-Making Process
- **Case Selection**:
  - **Writ of Certiorari**: The Court receives thousands of petitions annually but hears only a small percentage.
  - **Rule of Four**: At least four justices must agree to grant a review of a case.
- **Oral Arguments**:
  - **Public Sessions**: Attorneys present their cases and answer justices' questions.
- **Deliberations and Opinions**:
  - **Conference**: Justices discuss cases in private and vote.
  - **Opinion Writing**:
    - **Majority Opinion**: Reflects the Court's official ruling.
    - **Concurring Opinion**: Justices may agree with the decision but for different reasons.
    - **Dissenting Opinion**: Justices who disagree with the majority may write dissents.

Judicial Philosophies
- **Originalism**:
  - **Definition**: Interpreting the Constitution based on the framers' original intent.
  - **Advocates**: Justices like **Antonin Scalia** argued for this approach.
- **Living Constitution**:
  - **Definition**: Viewing the Constitution as a dynamic document that adapts to contemporary society.
  - **Advocates**: Justices like **Stephen Breyer** support this perspective.
- **Stare Decisis**:
  - **Definition**: The principle of adhering to precedent to ensure legal stability.
  - **Application**: The Court sometimes overturns precedent when deemed necessary.

Chapter 14: Constitutional Interpretation Methods

As you delve deeper into the workings of the United States Constitution, it's essential to understand how this living document is interpreted and applied to contemporary issues. The methods of constitutional interpretation play a crucial role in shaping legal outcomes and, by extension, American society. This chapter explores the various interpretative approaches used by jurists, scholars, and the Supreme Court, highlighting their principles, applications, and the debates surrounding them.

14.1 Introduction to Constitutional Interpretation

The Importance of Interpretation in Constitutional Law

The Constitution, while providing a foundational framework, contains language that can be broad, ambiguous, or silent on specific modern issues. Interpreting this document requires jurists to bridge the gap between the 18th-century text and 21st-century realities.

Role of the Supreme Court
- **Ultimate Interpreter**: The Supreme Court serves as the final authority on constitutional interpretation.
- **Balancing Act**: Justices must balance respect for the Constitution's text and intent with the need to address contemporary societal changes.

Challenges in Interpretation
- **Ambiguity and Generality**: Phrases like "due process" and "equal protection" require interpretation.
- **Changing Contexts**: Advances in technology, societal values, and international relations introduce new considerations.

Purpose of Interpretation Methods
- **Consistency**: Provide a framework for making judicial decisions.
- **Legitimacy**: Ensure that interpretations are grounded in accepted legal reasoning.
- **Predictability**: Offer guidance for future cases and legal understanding.

14.2 Textualism

Focusing on the Constitution's Plain Meaning

Textualism is an interpretative method that emphasizes the ordinary meaning of the Constitution's words at the time they were written.

Principles of Textualism
- **Plain Language**: Interprets the text based on the common understanding of the words.
- **Objective Approach**: Avoids inferring intent beyond the text.
- **Against Extrinsic Sources**: Minimizes reliance on legislative history or the framers' subjective intentions.

Key Advocates
- **Justice Hugo Black**: Known for his strict adherence to the text, especially regarding the First Amendment.
- **Justice Antonin Scalia**: A prominent modern textualist who argued for interpretation based on the text's original meaning.

Applications in Case Law
- **District of Columbia v. Heller (2008)**:
    - **Issue**: Right to bear arms under the Second Amendment.
    - **Majority Opinion**: Justice Scalia focused on the text's plain meaning to affirm an individual's right to possess firearms.

Advantages of Textualism
- **Limits Judicial Discretion**: Reduces the influence of personal biases.
- **Promotes Consistency**: Anchors interpretation to the text, fostering stability.

Critiques of Textualism
- **Context Ignored**: Critics argue that ignoring historical context and purpose can lead to narrow or unjust outcomes.
- **Ambiguities Remain**: The text alone may not resolve all interpretative challenges.

14.3 Originalism

Interpreting the Constitution Based on Original Understanding

Originalism seeks to interpret the Constitution according to the original understanding of the framers and the people at the time of its ratification.

Principles of Originalism
- **Historical Context**: Emphasizes the framers' intentions and the historical circumstances.
- **Fixed Meaning**: Belief that the Constitution's meaning does not change over time.
- **Opposition to Judicial Activism**: Cautions against judges inferring new rights not grounded in the original text.

Variants of Originalism
1. **Original Intent**: Focuses on the framers' subjective intentions.
2. **Original Public Meaning**: Considers how the text was publicly understood at the time.

Key Advocates
- **Justice Clarence Thomas**: Known for his originalist approach in constitutional interpretation.
- **Robert Bork**: A legal scholar and jurist who strongly advocated originalism.

Applications in Case Law
- **Brown v. Board of Education (1954)**:
  - **Originalist Challenge**: Critics argue that the framers of the Fourteenth Amendment did not intend to prohibit segregated schools.
  - **Court's Approach**: The decision relied more on the detrimental effects of segregation than on original intent.
- **Obergefell v. Hodges (2015)**:
  - **Originalist Dissents**: Justices Scalia and Thomas dissented, arguing that same-sex marriage was not contemplated by the framers.

Advantages of Originalism
- **Constrains Judicial Power**: Prevents judges from imposing personal values.
- **Democratic Legitimacy**: Respects decisions made by the Constitution's drafters and ratifiers.

Critiques of Originalism
- **Historical Limitations**: Difficulty in accurately determining original intent or public meaning.
- **Inflexibility**: May not accommodate societal changes or advancements.
- **Moral Concerns**: Original understandings may reflect outdated or unjust views.

14.4 Living Constitutionalism

Viewing the Constitution as a Dynamic Document
Living Constitutionalism posits that the Constitution's meaning can evolve over time to meet contemporary societal needs.

Principles of Living Constitutionalism
- **Adaptability**: The Constitution must be interpreted in the context of present-day values and realities.
- **Purposeful Interpretation**: Focuses on the underlying principles rather than fixed meanings.
- **Emphasis on Justice**: Aims to achieve equitable outcomes that align with modern understandings of rights.

Key Advocates
- **Justice William J. Brennan Jr.**: Articulated the need for a living Constitution responsive to societal progress.
- **Justice Stephen Breyer**: Promotes a pragmatic approach considering the Constitution's purposes.

Applications in Case Law
- **Roe v. Wade (1973)**:
  - **Right to Privacy**: Recognized a woman's right to choose abortion, expanding the interpretation of personal liberty.
- **Lawrence v. Texas (2003)**:
  - **Overturning Precedent**: Invalidated sodomy laws, reflecting evolving views on privacy and equality.

Advantages of Living Constitutionalism
- **Relevance**: Keeps the Constitution applicable to modern issues.
- **Progressive Change**: Facilitates the expansion of rights and protections.

Critiques of Living Constitutionalism
- **Judicial Overreach**: Critics argue it allows judges to create new rights based on personal beliefs.
- **Uncertainty**: May lead to unpredictability in legal interpretations.

14.5 Doctrinalism (Stare Decisis)

Reliance on Judicial Precedent
Doctrinalism emphasizes the importance of precedent, adhering to previous judicial decisions to guide interpretation.

Principles of Doctrinalism
- **Stare Decisis**: Latin for "to stand by things decided," promoting legal consistency.
- **Incremental Change**: Supports gradual legal development through case law.

Key Aspects
- **Legal Stability**: Provides predictability for individuals and institutions.
- **Judicial Efficiency**: Reduces the need to re-litigate settled issues.

Applications in Case Law

- **Plessy v. Ferguson (1896)** and **Brown v. Board of Education (1954)**:
  - **Overruling Precedent**: Brown overturned Plessy, demonstrating that precedents can change when deemed unjust.

Advantages of Doctrinalism
- **Consistency**: Ensures similar cases are treated alike.
- **Respect for Judicial Decisions**: Upholds the integrity of the legal system.

Critiques of Doctrinalism
- **Entrenchment of Injustice**: May perpetuate outdated or harmful rulings.
- **Resistance to Necessary Change**: Can slow the adaptation of the law to new realities.

14.6 Structuralism
Interpreting Based on the Constitution's Overall Structure

Structuralism looks at the Constitution's structures and relationships among its parts to derive meaning.

Principles of Structuralism
- **Holistic Approach**: Considers the Constitution's overall framework.
- **Implicit Principles**: Identifies underlying concepts like federalism and separation of powers.

Applications in Case Law
- **McCulloch v. Maryland (1819)**:
  - **Federal Supremacy**: Emphasized the structural relationship between federal and state governments.
- **Printz v. United States (1997)**:
  - **State Sovereignty**: Struck down federal mandates on states, highlighting the Constitution's structural protections of state autonomy.

Advantages of Structuralism
- **Coherent Interpretation**: Ensures consistency with the Constitution's design.
- **Protection of Fundamental Principles**: Reinforces essential governmental functions and relationships.

Critiques of Structuralism
- **Subjectivity**: Determining structural principles can be interpretative.
- **Limited Guidance**: May not address specific rights or issues directly.

14.7 Pragmatism
Considering Practical Consequences

Pragmatism involves interpreting the Constitution by evaluating the practical effects of legal decisions.

Principles of Pragmatism
- **Outcome-Oriented**: Focuses on the consequences of interpretations.
- **Balancing Interests**: Weighs individual rights against societal needs.
- **Flexibility**: Adapts legal reasoning to achieve beneficial results.

Key Advocates
- **Justice Oliver Wendell Holmes Jr.**: Emphasized the law's practical application over abstract principles.

Applications in Case Law
- **New York Times Co. v. United States (1971)**:
  - **Pentagon Papers Case**: Weighed the government's interest in national security against freedom of the press.
- **Kyllo v. United States (2001)**:
  - **Privacy and Technology**: Addressed the use of thermal imaging, considering implications for privacy rights.

Advantages of Pragmatism
- **Real-World Relevance**: Decisions are grounded in current societal contexts.
- **Problem-Solving**: Seeks to address legal issues effectively.

Critiques of Pragmatism
- **Unpredictability**: May lead to inconsistent rulings.
- **Judicial Activism**: Critics argue it allows judges too much discretion.

14.8 Ethical Interpretation
Infusing Moral Philosophy into Constitutional Meaning

Ethical Interpretation involves applying moral reasoning and fundamental ethical principles to constitutional interpretation.

Principles of Ethical Interpretation
- **Moral Readings**: Considers justice, human dignity, and moral values.
- **Universal Principles**: Applies concepts like equality and fairness.

Key Advocates

- **Justice Thurgood Marshall**: Advocated for interpretations that promote justice and equality.
- **Ronald Dworkin**: A legal philosopher who emphasized "law as integrity," integrating moral principles.

Applications in Case Law
- **Furman v. Georgia (1972)**:
  - **Death Penalty**: Considered the morality of capital punishment under the Eighth Amendment.
- **Roper v. Simmons (2005)**:
  - **Juvenile Death Penalty**: Ruled it unconstitutional to execute individuals for crimes committed as minors.

Advantages of Ethical Interpretation
- **Promotes Justice**: Aims to align the law with ethical standards.
- **Addresses Moral Issues**: Tackles complex social and moral dilemmas.

Critiques of Ethical Interpretation
- **Subjectivity**: Moral values can vary, leading to differing conclusions.
- **Judicial Overreach**: Potentially allows judges to impose personal moral views.

14.9 Debates and Implications

The Ongoing Discourse on Interpretation Methods

The choice of interpretative method significantly influences judicial decisions, affecting legislation, individual rights, and societal norms.

Judicial Philosophy and Court Dynamics
- **Influence on Case Outcomes**: Justices' interpretative approaches can lead to divergent rulings on similar issues.
- **Court Composition**: The balance of interpretative philosophies among justices shapes the Court's direction.

Political and Social Implications
- **Policy Impact**: Court decisions can validate or invalidate laws, affecting policy implementation.
- **Public Perception**: The legitimacy of the Court can be influenced by perceptions of judicial activism or restraint.

Balancing Methods
- **Hybrid Approaches**: Justices may combine methods, considering text, intent, precedent, and consequences.
- **Adaptation Over Time**: Interpretative methods evolve, reflecting changes in legal thought and societal values.

Educational and Professional Importance
- **Legal Education**: Understanding interpretation methods is essential for law students and practitioners.
- **Advocacy and Litigation**: Lawyers tailor arguments to resonate with justices' interpretative preferences.

Chapter 15: Ongoing Constitutional Debates

As you continue your exploration of the United States Constitution, it becomes evident that this living document remains at the center of many contemporary legal and political debates. The Constitution's enduring relevance is both a testament to its foundational principles and a reflection of the evolving challenges faced by American society. In this chapter, we'll examine some of the most pressing ongoing constitutional debates, exploring the complexities and differing perspectives that shape these discussions.

15.1 The Second Amendment and Gun Control

Balancing the Right to Bear Arms with Public Safety

The **Second Amendment** states:

"A well regulated Militia, being necessary to the security of a free State, the right of the people to keep and bear Arms, shall not be infringed."

The Debate Overview

- **Gun Rights Advocates**:
  - **Individual Right**: Emphasize the Supreme Court's recognition of an individual's right to possess firearms, as affirmed in **District of Columbia v. Heller (2008)**.
  - **Self-Defense and Liberty**: Argue that firearms are essential for personal protection and as a safeguard against tyranny.
  - **Opposition to Regulation**: Resist laws perceived as infringing upon the Second Amendment.
- **Gun Control Advocates**:
  - **Public Safety Concerns**: Highlight the high rates of gun violence, mass shootings, and accidental deaths.
  - **Regulation Support**: Advocate for measures like background checks, assault weapons bans, and red flag laws.
  - **Interpretation of "Well Regulated Militia"**: Argue that the framers intended regulated firearm ownership connected to militia service.

Legal and Constitutional Considerations

- **Supreme Court Decisions**:
  - **McDonald v. City of Chicago (2010)**: Incorporated the Second Amendment to apply to state and local governments.
  - **New York State Rifle & Pistol Association Inc. v. Bruen (2022)**: Struck down restrictive concealed carry laws, reinforcing individual rights.
- **Legislative Actions**:
  - **Federal and State Laws**: Varied regulations across states create a patchwork of gun laws.
  - **Recent Legislation**: Efforts to enact universal background checks and other measures face political hurdles.

Ongoing Challenges

- **Balancing Rights and Safety**: Finding common ground between protecting constitutional rights and reducing gun violence remains contentious.
- **Cultural Factors**: Firearms hold significant cultural importance for many Americans, complicating policy discussions.
- **Technological Advancements**: The rise of 3D-printed guns and ghost guns introduces new regulatory challenges.

15.2 First Amendment in the Digital Age

Free Speech, Social Media, and Misinformation

The **First Amendment** protects freedoms of speech, press, assembly, religion, and petition. In the digital era, these rights intersect with new platforms and technologies.

The Debate Overview

- **Freedom of Expression**:
  - **Protecting Speech Online**: Advocates emphasize that the internet is a modern public square where free speech must be upheld.
  - **Opposition to Censorship**: Concerns over government or corporate suppression of viewpoints.
- **Combatting Misinformation and Hate Speech**:
  - **Public Harm**: Misinformation can impact public health (e.g., during

pandemics) and democratic processes.
- o **Regulation Support**: Calls for platforms to moderate content to prevent the spread of harmful or false information.

Legal and Constitutional Considerations
- **Section 230 of the Communications Decency Act (1996)**:
  - o **Liability Shield**: Protects online platforms from being held liable for user-generated content.
  - o **Debate**: Discussions about reforming or repealing Section 230 to hold platforms accountable.
- **Supreme Court Cases**:
  - o **Packingham v. North Carolina (2017)**: Recognized social media as a critical space for free expression.
  - o **Mahanoy Area School District v. B.L. (2021)**: Addressed student speech on social media outside of school grounds.

Ongoing Challenges
- **Defining Limits**: Determining when speech crosses into unprotected categories like incitement or defamation.
- **Platform Responsibility**: Balancing free speech with the responsibility of tech companies to manage content.
- **Global Implications**: International laws and norms influence how platforms operate and regulate speech.

15.3 Privacy Rights and Surveillance
The Fourth Amendment in an Age of Technology
The **Fourth Amendment** protects against unreasonable searches and seizures, ensuring privacy and security.

The Debate Overview
- **Privacy Advocates**:
  - o **Protection from Surveillance**: Concern over government and corporate collection of personal data.
  - o **Digital Privacy**: Emphasize the need to update legal protections to address modern technologies.
- **Security and Law Enforcement**:
  - o **National Security**: Surveillance is seen as essential for preventing terrorism and crime.
  - o **Legal Tools**: Authorities argue for access to data to effectively enforce laws.

Legal and Constitutional Considerations
- **Supreme Court Decisions**:
  - o **Katz v. United States (1967)**: Established the "reasonable expectation of privacy" standard.
  - o **Carpenter v. United States (2018)**: Required law enforcement to obtain warrants to access cell phone location data.
- **Legislation**:
  - o **Patriot Act (2001)**: Expanded surveillance capabilities post-9/11, raising privacy concerns.
  - o **USA Freedom Act (2015)**: Implemented reforms but debates over government surveillance persist.

Ongoing Challenges
- **Technological Advancements**: Facial recognition, drones, and AI introduce new privacy considerations.
- **Data Collection by Corporations**: The role of private companies in collecting and sharing user data.
- **Encryption and Law Enforcement Access**: Balancing privacy with the need for authorities to access encrypted communications.

15.4 Federalism and States' Rights
The Balance of Power Between Federal and State Governments
Federalism remains a core feature of the U.S. constitutional system, with ongoing debates about the appropriate division of powers.

The Debate Overview
- **States' Rights Advocates**:
  - o **Local Control**: Emphasize the importance of state autonomy in areas like education, healthcare, and criminal justice.
  - o **Resistance to Federal Overreach**: Challenge federal mandates perceived as infringing on state sovereignty.
- **Federal Authority Advocates**:
  - o **National Standards**: Argue for uniform policies to address issues

like civil rights, environmental protection, and healthcare.
  - **Supremacy Clause**: Highlight that federal laws supersede conflicting state laws.

Legal and Constitutional Considerations
- **Supreme Court Decisions**:
  - **Arizona v. United States (2012)**: Limited state authority in immigration enforcement.
  - **NFIB v. Sebelius (2012)**: Addressed federal power in healthcare mandates under the Affordable Care Act.
- **Contemporary Issues**:
  - **Marijuana Legalization**: States legalizing cannabis despite federal prohibition.
  - **Sanctuary Cities**: Local jurisdictions limiting cooperation with federal immigration enforcement.

Ongoing Challenges
- **Policy Innovation vs. Uniformity**: Balancing states as "laboratories of democracy" with the need for national coherence.
- **Preemption and Conflicts**: Navigating areas where state and federal laws directly conflict.
- **Political Polarization**: Increasing ideological divides between states amplify federalism debates.

15.5 Electoral College and Voting Rights

Debates Over Democratic Representation and Election Integrity

The mechanisms of American democracy, including the **Electoral College** and voting rights, are subjects of intense debate.

The Electoral College Debate
- **Critics**:
  - **Undemocratic Outcomes**: Instances where candidates win the popular vote but lose the electoral vote.
  - **Disproportionate Influence**: Smaller states and swing states have outsized impact on elections.
- **Supporters**:
  - **Federalist Principles**: Designed to balance interests of states with varying populations.
  - **Stability**: Argue that it contributes to political stability by requiring widespread support.

Voting Rights and Access
- **Expansion Advocates**:
  - **Voter Accessibility**: Support measures like early voting, mail-in ballots, and same-day registration.
  - **Opposition to Voter ID Laws**: Argue such laws suppress turnout among marginalized groups.
- **Election Integrity Advocates**:
  - **Preventing Fraud**: Emphasize the need for secure elections through measures like voter ID requirements.
  - **Voter Roll Maintenance**: Support purging outdated registrations to prevent irregularities.

Legal and Constitutional Considerations
- **Supreme Court Decisions**:
  - **Shelby County v. Holder (2013)**: Struck down key provisions of the Voting Rights Act, affecting federal oversight of state election laws.
  - **Bush v. Gore (2000)**: Resolved a disputed presidential election, highlighting electoral system complexities.
- **Legislation**:
  - **For the People Act**: Proposed federal standards for elections, facing partisan debate.
  - **John Lewis Voting Rights Advancement Act**: Aims to restore and strengthen protections against discriminatory voting practices.

Ongoing Challenges
- **Gerrymandering**: Manipulation of electoral district boundaries for partisan gain.
- **Electoral Reform Proposals**: Suggestions include abolishing the Electoral College or adopting the National Popular Vote Interstate Compact.
- **Ensuring Fair Access**: Balancing security measures with the protection of voting rights for all citizens.

15.6 Supreme Court Composition and Tenure

Debates Over Judicial Appointments and Court Structure

The composition and functioning of the **Supreme Court** are subjects of ongoing discussion, particularly regarding lifetime appointments and the Court's size.

Appointment Process Concerns
- **Partisan Confirmation Battles**:
  - **Political Polarization**: Nominations and confirmations have become highly contentious.
  - **Impact on Judicial Independence**: Concerns that justices are viewed as political actors.
- **Timing of Appointments**:
  - **Election Year Nominations**: Debates over confirming justices during presidential election years.

Proposals for Reform
- **Term Limits**:
  - **Fixed Terms**: Suggestions to limit justices' terms to promote regular turnover and reduce politicization.
  - **Constitutional Considerations**: Implementing term limits may require a constitutional amendment.
- **Court Expansion ("Court Packing")**:
  - **Increasing the Number of Justices**: Proposed to rebalance the Court ideologically.
  - **Historical Precedent**: FDR's unsuccessful attempt in the 1930s.
- **Mandatory Retirement Ages**:
  - **Age Limits**: Instituting a retirement age to ensure consistent opportunities for new appointments.

Legal and Constitutional Considerations
- **Article III**: Provides for lifetime tenure "during good behavior," ensuring judicial independence.
- **Congressional Authority**: Congress has the power to change the Court's size, as it has in the past.

Ongoing Challenges
- **Maintaining Legitimacy**: Ensuring the Court is perceived as an impartial arbiter of the law.
- **Balancing Independence and Accountability**: Protecting justices from political pressures while promoting transparency.
- **Addressing Public Confidence**: Polls indicate varying levels of trust in the judiciary, impacting its authority.

15.7 The Role of Money in Politics

Campaign Finance, Free Speech, and Democratic Participation

The influence of money in political campaigns raises questions about corruption, free speech, and equality.

The Debate Overview
- **Campaign Finance Reform Advocates**:
  - **Reducing Influence**: Aim to limit the impact of wealthy individuals and corporations on elections.
  - **Transparency**: Support disclosure of donors and spending.
- **Free Speech Advocates**:
  - **First Amendment Rights**: Argue that spending money on political speech is a protected expression.
  - **Opposition to Limits**: Believe restrictions infringe on constitutional freedoms.

Legal and Constitutional Considerations
- **Supreme Court Decisions**:
  - **Buckley v. Valeo (1976)**: Upheld limits on campaign contributions but not on independent expenditures.
  - **Citizens United v. FEC (2010)**:
    - **Decision**: Held that corporate funding of independent political broadcasts cannot be limited.
    - **Impact**: Led to the rise of Super PACs and increased outside spending.
- **Legislation**:
  - **Bipartisan Campaign Reform Act (2002)**: Sought to regulate campaign financing, parts of which were invalidated by Citizens United.

Ongoing Challenges
- **Dark Money**: Anonymous funding in politics raises concerns about accountability.
- **Inequality of Influence**: Wealthy donors may have disproportionate impact on political outcomes.

- **Efforts for Reform**: Proposals include constitutional amendments to overturn Citizens United or public financing of campaigns.

15.8 Equal Rights Amendment and Gender Equality

Renewed Efforts to Enshrine Gender Equality in the Constitution

The **Equal Rights Amendment (ERA)** seeks to guarantee equal legal rights regardless of sex.

The Debate Overview
- **Supporters**:
  - **Constitutional Guarantee**: Argue that explicit protection is necessary to ensure gender equality.
  - **Legal Consistency**: Believe the ERA would strengthen enforcement of laws against gender discrimination.
- **Opponents**:
  - **Redundancy**: Claim existing laws and the Fourteenth Amendment already provide protections.
  - **Unintended Consequences**: Concerns about impacts on issues like abortion rights and gender-specific accommodations.

Legal and Constitutional Considerations
- **Ratification Status**:
  - **Historical Context**: Passed by Congress in 1972, but failed to achieve ratification by the 1982 deadline.
  - **Recent Developments**: Additional states have ratified in recent years, sparking legal debates over validity.
- **Legislative Actions**:
  - **Deadline Removal**: Efforts in Congress to eliminate the ratification deadline.
  - **Department of Justice Opinions**: Legal interpretations vary on whether the ERA can still be ratified.

Ongoing Challenges
- **Legal Uncertainty**: Courts may need to resolve questions about the ratification process.
- **Continued Gender Disparities**: Wage gaps, representation in leadership, and discrimination persist.
- **Advocacy and Awareness**: Movements like #MeToo have highlighted ongoing issues of gender equality.

15.9 Immigration and Constitutional Rights

Navigating Federal Authority and Individual Protections

Immigration policy raises constitutional questions about federal power, due process, and equal protection.

The Debate Overview
- **Immigration Enforcement**:
  - **National Security and Sovereignty**: Emphasis on controlling borders and enforcing immigration laws.
  - **Executive Authority**: Use of executive orders to implement policies.
- **Immigrant Rights Advocates**:
  - **Due Process Protections**: Argue that all persons, regardless of status, are entitled to constitutional protections.
  - **Humanitarian Concerns**: Focus on family separation, asylum seekers, and detention conditions.

Legal and Constitutional Considerations
- **Supreme Court Decisions**:
  - **Plyler v. Doe (1982)**: Struck down a state law denying public education to undocumented children.
  - **Department of Homeland Security v. Regents of the University of California (2020)**: Addressed the rescission of the Deferred Action for Childhood Arrivals (DACA) program.
- **Executive Actions**:
  - **Travel Bans**: Legal challenges to restrictions on entry from certain countries.
  - **Border Policies**: Debates over the legality and morality of measures like family separation.

Chapter 16: The Constitution's Global Influence

The United States Constitution, as one of the oldest written constitutions still in use, has had a profound impact beyond American borders. Its principles, structures, and ideas have influenced the development of constitutions around the world, inspiring movements toward democracy, human rights, and the rule of law. In this chapter, we'll explore how the U.S. Constitution has shaped global constitutionalism, examining its direct influences, adaptations by other nations, and its role in international law and governance.

16.1 The Spread of Constitutionalism

The Rise of Written Constitutions Worldwide

The concept of a written constitution as a foundational legal document originated with the U.S. Constitution in 1787. Prior to this, most nations operated under unwritten constitutions, customary laws, or monarchies with absolute power.

Influence on Early Constitutions

- **France and the French Revolution (1789-1799):**
    - **Declaration of the Rights of Man and of the Citizen (1789):** Echoed principles from the U.S. Declaration of Independence and Constitution, emphasizing individual rights and popular sovereignty.
    - **Constitution of 1791:** Established a constitutional monarchy, influenced by the separation of powers outlined in the U.S. Constitution.
- **Poland-Lithuania:**
    - **Constitution of May 3, 1791:** Europe's first modern constitution, reflecting Enlightenment ideas and inspired by American constitutionalism.

19th Century Constitutional Movements

- **Latin America:**
    - **Post-Independence Constitutions:** Newly independent nations like Mexico (1824) and Colombia (1819) crafted constitutions incorporating U.S. constitutional principles, including federalism and checks and balances.
    - **Simón Bolívar:** Admired the U.S. system and advocated for republican governance in South America.
- **Europe:**
    - **Constitutional Monarchies:** Nations like Belgium (1831) and Norway (1814) adopted constitutions that balanced monarchic and democratic elements, influenced by the U.S. model.

20th Century Developments

- **Post-World War I and II:**
    - **Democratization:** The collapse of empires led to new nations adopting constitutions with democratic principles.
    - **Weimar Republic (Germany, 1919):** Included a bill of rights and parliamentary democracy, reflecting U.S. constitutional ideas.
- **Decolonization Era:**
    - **Africa and Asia:** Newly independent countries often looked to the U.S. Constitution as a template for nation-building and governance structures.

16.2 Core Principles and Their Global Adoption

Key Constitutional Concepts and Their International Influence

The U.S. Constitution introduced several foundational principles that have been widely adopted and adapted by other nations.

Separation of Powers

- **Concept:** Dividing government into distinct branches (legislative, executive, judicial) to prevent concentration of power.
- **Global Adoption:**
    - **France's Fifth Republic (1958):** Established a semi-presidential system with clear separation of powers.
    - **India's Constitution (1950):** Embraced separation of powers within a parliamentary system.

Federalism

- **Concept:** A system where power is divided between a central government and regional governments.

- **Global Adoption**:
  - **Canada**:
    - **British North America Act (1867)**: Created a federal dominion, balancing powers between federal and provincial governments.
  - **Australia**:
    - **Constitution of 1901**: Established a federal system influenced by the U.S. model.
  - **Germany**:
    - **Basic Law (1949)**: Implemented federalism to distribute power and prevent central authoritarianism.

Judicial Review
- **Concept**: The judiciary's power to review and invalidate legislative and executive actions that violate the constitution.
- **Global Adoption**:
  - **Marbury v. Madison Influence**: Many countries established constitutional courts with the authority to interpret the constitution.
  - **Germany's Federal Constitutional Court**: Has significant power to review legislation.
  - **India's Supreme Court**: Exercises judicial review to uphold constitutional provisions.

Bill of Rights and Individual Liberties
- **Concept**: Enumerated rights protecting individuals from government infringement.
- **Global Adoption**:
  - **Universal Declaration of Human Rights (1948)**:
    - **Influence**: The U.S. Bill of Rights inspired international human rights norms.
  - **South Africa's Constitution (1996)**:
    - **Comprehensive Bill of Rights**: Enshrines civil, political, and socio-economic rights.
  - **European Convention on Human Rights (1950)**:
    - **Regional Protections**: Provides a framework for member states to protect individual rights.

16.3 Case Studies of Constitutional Influence

Specific Examples of Countries Drawing from the U.S. Constitution

India
- **Constitution of 1950**:
  - **Democratic Framework**: Adopted principles of federalism, fundamental rights, and judicial review.
  - **Adaptations**:
    - **Parliamentary System**: Combined U.S. constitutional principles with British parliamentary traditions.
    - **Directive Principles**: Introduced socio-economic guidelines for the state, expanding beyond the U.S. model.

Japan
- **Post-War Constitution (1947)**:
  - **U.S. Involvement**: Drafted under the guidance of the Allied occupation, particularly General Douglas MacArthur.
  - **Key Features**:
    - **Demilitarization**: Article 9 renounces war, a unique provision not present in the U.S. Constitution.
    - **Democratic Governance**: Established parliamentary democracy, fundamental rights, and separation of powers.

Germany
- **Basic Law (Grundgesetz) of 1949**:
  - **Federal Structure**: Emphasized federalism to prevent centralization of power, learning from the Weimar Republic's weaknesses.
  - **Human Rights**:
    - **Inviolable Rights**: Strong protections for human dignity and individual freedoms.
  - **Constitutional Court**:

- **Judicial Review**: Modeled after the U.S. Supreme Court's role in constitutional interpretation.

South Africa
- **Post-Apartheid Constitution (1996)**:
  - **Inclusive Process**: Developed through extensive public participation and negotiation.
  - **Borrowed Principles**:
    - **Bill of Rights**: Comprehensive protections, influenced by the U.S. Bill of Rights and international human rights law.
    - **Constitutional Court**: Empowered to enforce constitutional provisions and rights.

Latin America
- **Mexico's Constitution (1917)**:
  - **Revolutionary Ideas**: Included social rights, land reform, and labor rights, expanding upon U.S. constitutional concepts.
  - **Federalism**: Adopted a federal structure similar to the U.S., with adaptations for local contexts.
- **Brazil's Constitution (1988)**:
  - **Democratic Restoration**: After military rule, embraced democratic governance with a strong emphasis on social rights.
  - **Judicial Review**: Established mechanisms for constitutional interpretation and protection of rights.

16.4 The Constitution and International Law

Influence on International Organizations and Legal Norms

The U.S. Constitution's principles have extended into the realm of international law and organizations.

United Nations Charter (1945)
- **Foundational Principles**:
  - **Human Rights**: The U.N. Charter emphasizes the promotion of human rights, reflecting U.S. constitutional values.
  - **Rule of Law**: Encourages peaceful resolution of disputes and adherence to international law.

Universal Declaration of Human Rights (1948)
- **Eleanor Roosevelt's Role**:
  - **Leadership**: As chair of the drafting committee, she influenced the inclusion of civil and political rights reminiscent of the U.S. Bill of Rights.
- **Global Standards**:
  - **Comprehensive Rights**: Encompasses rights to life, liberty, security, and freedom of expression.

International Criminal Court (ICC)
- **Judicial Principles**:
  - **Due Process Rights**: Procedures and protections in the ICC reflect fair trial standards similar to those in the U.S. Constitution.

Democracy Promotion
- **U.S. Foreign Policy**:
  - **Support for Democratic Institutions**: The U.S. has historically promoted constitutional governance and human rights abroad.
- **International Aid and Advising**:
  - **Constitutional Assistance**: U.S. experts have assisted in drafting constitutions for emerging democracies.

16.5 Adaptations and Divergences

How Other Nations Have Modified Constitutional Principles

While many countries have drawn inspiration from the U.S. Constitution, they have also adapted its principles to fit their unique historical, cultural, and social contexts.

Parliamentary Systems
- **Preference Over Presidential Systems**:
  - **United Kingdom Influence**: Many former British colonies adopted parliamentary systems, valuing the fusion of executive and legislative powers.
- **Adaptation**:
  - **Checks and Balances**: Incorporated mechanisms to prevent abuse of power, even within a parliamentary framework.

Extended Rights Protections
- **Socio-Economic Rights**:
  - **Beyond Civil Liberties**: Constitutions like South Africa's include rights to housing, healthcare, and education.
- **Group Rights**:
  - **Cultural and Minority Protections**: Some constitutions recognize collective rights, addressing diverse populations.

Constitutional Amendment Processes
- **Flexibility vs. Rigidity**:
  - **Easier Amendment Procedures**: Some countries allow for more accessible constitutional changes to adapt to evolving needs.
  - **Entrenched Clauses**: Others include unamendable provisions to protect fundamental principles.

Judicial Structures
- **Specialized Constitutional Courts**:
  - **Separate from Supreme Courts**: Many nations have distinct constitutional courts solely for constitutional matters.
- **Appointment Processes**:
  - **Varied Methods**: Judges may be appointed by different branches or bodies to ensure independence and representation.

16.6 Critiques and Challenges of Constitutional Transplants

Limitations and Criticisms of Applying U.S. Constitutional Models Abroad

While the U.S. Constitution has been influential, applying its principles in other contexts has not been without challenges.

Cultural and Historical Differences
- **Incompatibility with Local Traditions**:
  - **Legal Systems**: Countries with civil law traditions may find common law principles less applicable.
  - **Societal Values**: Concepts like individualism may clash with communal cultures.

Implementation Difficulties
- **Institutional Capacity**:
  - **Lack of Resources**: New democracies may struggle to establish effective institutions.
- **Political Instability**:
  - **Frequent Changes**: Some countries experience constitutional amendments or replacements due to coups or regime changes.

Perceived Imposition
- **Neo-Colonial Critiques**:
  - **External Influence**: Resistance to constitutional models seen as imposed by foreign powers.
- **Legitimacy Issues**:
  - **Public Buy-In**: Successful constitutions often require widespread public participation and acceptance.

Adaptation Necessity
- **One Size Does Not Fit All**:
  - **Customization Required**: Constitutions must reflect a nation's specific needs, challenges, and aspirations.
- **Learning from U.S. Challenges**:
  - **Avoiding Pitfalls**: Other nations may seek to address issues like systemic racism or electoral complexities observed in the U.S.

16.7 The Constitution in the Modern Global Context

The U.S. Constitution's Role in Contemporary International Affairs

In today's interconnected world, the U.S. Constitution continues to be a reference point in global discussions about governance, rights, and democracy.

Human Rights Advocacy
- **Global Movements**:
  - **Civil Liberties**: Activists worldwide draw upon the U.S. civil rights movement and constitutional protections.
- **Internet Freedom**:
  - **First Amendment Influence**: The U.S. stance on free speech informs international debates on digital expression.

Democracy Promotion and Challenges
- **U.S. Leadership Role:**
  - **Advocacy:** The U.S. promotes democratic principles through diplomacy and international organizations.
- **Perceptions Abroad:**
  - **Critiques of U.S. Practices:** International observers may point to issues like political polarization or social injustice as challenges to the U.S. model.

Transnational Legal Influence
- **Constitutional Dialogue:**
  - **Judicial References:** Courts in other countries sometimes cite U.S. Supreme Court decisions.
- **Legal Education:**
  - **Academic Exchanges:** U.S. constitutional law is studied globally, influencing legal scholars and practitioners.

Global Constitutionalism
- **Shared Challenges:**
  - **Balancing Security and Liberty:** Nations grapple with similar issues, such as counterterrorism measures and privacy rights.
- **Collaborative Efforts:**
  - **International Agreements:** Treaties and conventions reflect constitutional principles on human rights and governance.

Chapter 17: Civic Responsibility

In the journey through the United States Constitution and its profound impact on the nation's history and governance, it is essential to recognize the role of **civic responsibility** in sustaining and nurturing the democratic ideals enshrined in this foundational document. Civic responsibility refers to the duties and obligations of citizens to actively participate in the political and community life of their society. This chapter explores the various facets of civic responsibility, emphasizing the importance of informed engagement, respect for the rule of law, and contributions to the common good.

17.1 Understanding Civic Responsibility

The Foundation of Active Citizenship
Civic responsibility is rooted in the concept of **citizenship**, which encompasses not only the rights and privileges granted by the Constitution and laws but also the obligations individuals have toward their community and nation.

Definition and Scope
- **Civic Responsibility**: The commitment of citizens to engage in actions and behaviors that contribute positively to society and support democratic governance.
- **Active Participation**: Involvement in activities that influence public policy, community well-being, and the functioning of government.

Key Components
1. **Knowledge of Rights and Duties**:
   - **Constitutional Awareness**: Understanding the rights protected by the Constitution, such as freedom of speech, religion, and assembly.
   - **Legal Obligations**: Recognizing duties like obeying laws, paying taxes, and serving on juries.
2. **Community Involvement**:
   - **Volunteering**: Offering time and skills to support community initiatives and address local needs.
   - **Civic Engagement**: Participating in public meetings, local governance, and community organizations.
3. **Political Participation**:
   - **Voting**: Exercising the right to vote in elections to choose representatives and influence policies.
   - **Advocacy**: Engaging in dialogue, campaigning, and lobbying for issues of concern.
4. **Respect for the Rule of Law**:
   - **Legal Compliance**: Adhering to laws and regulations that govern society.
   - **Justice Promotion**: Supporting fair treatment and equality under the law.

Importance of Civic Responsibility
- **Sustaining Democracy**: Active citizen participation is essential for a healthy democracy, ensuring that government reflects the people's will.
- **Community Improvement**: Collective efforts address social issues, enhance quality of life, and promote social cohesion.
- **Protecting Rights**: Vigilant citizens help safeguard constitutional rights and freedoms against infringement.

17.2 The Role of Voting

Exercising the Fundamental Right to Vote
Voting is one of the most direct and impactful ways citizens can participate in their government. It is both a right and a responsibility that empowers individuals to shape public policy and leadership.

Historical Context
- **Expansion of Suffrage**:
  - **Early Limitations**: Initially, voting rights were restricted to white male property owners.
  - **Progressive Amendments**:
    - **Fifteenth Amendment (1870)**: Prohibited voting restrictions based on race.
    - **Nineteenth Amendment (1920)**: Granted women the right to vote.
    - **Twenty-Fourth Amendment (1964)**: Abolished poll taxes.
    - **Twenty-Sixth Amendment (1971)**: Lowered the voting age to 18.
- **Civil Rights Movement**:

- **Voting Rights Act of 1965**: Eliminated discriminatory practices that disenfranchised African Americans and other minorities.

The Importance of Voting
- **Democratic Legitimacy**: High voter participation ensures that elected officials represent the electorate's interests.
- **Policy Influence**: Voters can support candidates and initiatives that align with their values and priorities.
- **Accountability**: Regular elections allow citizens to hold public officials accountable for their actions and decisions.

Challenges to Voter Participation
- **Voter Apathy**: Lack of interest or belief that one's vote does not make a difference.
- **Barriers to Voting**:
  - **Registration Hurdles**: Complex registration processes can discourage participation.
  - **Accessibility Issues**: Physical barriers, lack of transportation, or limited polling hours can impede voting.
  - **Voter Suppression**: Laws or practices that intentionally or unintentionally disenfranchise certain groups.

Encouraging Voter Engagement
- **Education and Awareness**:
  - **Civic Education**: Teaching about the electoral process and the impact of voting.
  - **Information Access**: Providing resources on candidates, issues, and voting procedures.
- **Facilitating Access**:
  - **Online Registration**: Simplifying the registration process through digital means.
  - **Early and Mail-In Voting**: Offering flexible options to accommodate diverse needs.
- **Community Initiatives**:
  - **Voter Drives**: Organized efforts to register and mobilize voters.
  - **Peer Encouragement**: Individuals motivating friends and family to participate.

17.3 Jury Duty and the Judicial System

Participating in the Administration of Justice
Serving on a jury is a civic duty that allows citizens to play a direct role in the judicial system, ensuring fair trials and upholding the principle of justice.

The Right to a Jury Trial
- **Constitutional Guarantees**:
  - **Sixth Amendment**: Guarantees the right to a speedy and public trial by an impartial jury in criminal prosecutions.
  - **Seventh Amendment**: Preserves the right to a jury trial in federal civil cases exceeding a certain value.

Importance of Jury Service
- **Community Representation**: Juries composed of peers provide diverse perspectives, reflecting the community's values.
- **Checks and Balances**: Jurors act as a check on government power, safeguarding against unjust prosecutions.
- **Civic Engagement**: Serving on a jury fosters an understanding of the legal system and reinforces the rule of law.

Responsibilities of Jurors
- **Impartiality**: Jurors must evaluate evidence objectively, without bias or prejudice.
- **Confidentiality**: Maintaining the confidentiality of deliberations to protect the integrity of the process.
- **Duty to Serve**: Responding to summons and fulfilling the obligation unless excused for valid reasons.

Challenges and Considerations
- **Accessibility**:
  - **Hardships**: Financial or personal hardships may make jury service burdensome.
  - **Accommodations**: Courts often provide support, such as compensation or scheduling flexibility.
- **Diversity in Juries**:
  - **Representation Gaps**: Efforts are ongoing to ensure that juries reflect the diversity of the community.
  - **Elimination of Bias**: Legal safeguards aim to prevent discrimination in jury selection.

17.4 Obeying Laws and Paying Taxes
Supporting the Functioning of Government and Society
Compliance with laws and fulfilling financial obligations are fundamental aspects of civic responsibility that contribute to social order and public services.

Obeying Laws
- **Social Contract**: Citizens agree to abide by laws in exchange for protection and benefits provided by the government.
- **Maintaining Order**: Law adherence ensures safety, security, and the smooth functioning of society.
- **Legal Consequences**: Violations can result in penalties, affecting individuals and the broader community.

Paying Taxes
- **Funding Public Services**:
    - **Infrastructure**: Roads, bridges, public transportation.
    - **Education**: Public schools, libraries.
    - **Healthcare**: Public hospitals, health initiatives.
    - **Safety and Security**: Police, fire departments, military.
- **Fairness and Equity**:
    - **Progressive Taxation**: Higher earners contribute a larger share to support societal needs.
    - **Redistribution**: Taxes fund social programs that aid vulnerable populations.

Ethical Considerations
- **Tax Compliance**:
    - **Legal Obligations**: Filing accurate returns and paying due amounts.
    - **Avoiding Evasion**: Engaging in tax evasion undermines public trust and resources.
- **Civic Pride**:
    - **Contributing to the Common Good**: Recognizing taxes as an investment in the nation's future.
    - **Accountability**: Advocating for responsible government spending.

17.5 Community Involvement and Volunteering
Enhancing Society Through Active Participation
Beyond legal obligations, civic responsibility encompasses voluntary actions that improve communities and support those in need.

Forms of Community Involvement
- **Volunteering**:
    - **Nonprofits and Charities**: Assisting organizations that address social issues.
    - **Local Initiatives**: Participating in neighborhood clean-ups, food drives, or mentoring programs.
- **Civic Organizations**:
    - **Service Clubs**: Joining groups like Rotary, Lions, or Kiwanis that focus on community service.
    - **Advocacy Groups**: Engaging with organizations that promote causes such as environmental protection or human rights.
- **Public Participation**:
    - **Attending Meetings**: Being present at city council, school board, or town hall meetings.
    - **Public Comment**: Providing input on policies and community projects.

Benefits of Community Involvement
- **Strengthening Communities**: Collective efforts address local needs and foster solidarity.
- **Personal Growth**:
    - **Skill Development**: Gaining experience in leadership, communication, and problem-solving.
    - **Networking**: Building relationships with diverse individuals.
- **Civic Empowerment**: Empowering individuals to effect change and influence decisions.

Encouraging Involvement
- **Education**:
    - **Service Learning**: Integrating community service into educational curricula.
    - **Civic Education**: Teaching the value and impact of community participation.
- **Workplace Initiatives**:

- o **Corporate Social Responsibility**: Companies encouraging employee volunteering.
- o **Community Partnerships**: Collaborations between businesses and local organizations.

17.6 Civic Education and Informed Citizenship

The Importance of Knowledge and Critical Thinking

An informed citizenry is essential for a functioning democracy. Civic education equips individuals with the knowledge and skills needed to participate effectively.

Components of Civic Education
- **Understanding Government**:
    - o **Structures and Functions**: Learning how local, state, and federal governments operate.
    - o **Political Processes**: Understanding elections, legislative procedures, and policy-making.
- **Constitutional Knowledge**:
    - o **Rights and Liberties**: Familiarity with constitutional protections and how they apply.
    - o **Historical Context**: Awareness of the nation's founding principles and key historical events.
- **Critical Thinking**:
    - o **Media Literacy**: Evaluating sources for credibility and bias.
    - o **Analytical Skills**: Assessing arguments, identifying logical fallacies, and forming reasoned opinions.

Promoting Civic Education
- **Formal Education**:
    - o **Curriculum Integration**: Incorporating civics, history, and social studies in school programs.
    - o **Experiential Learning**: Field trips, mock elections, and debates.
- **Public Resources**:
    - o **Libraries and Museums**: Offering programs and exhibits on civic topics.
    - o **Online Platforms**: Providing accessible educational content and tools.
- **Community Programs**:
    - o **Workshops and Seminars**: Hosting events to discuss current issues and civic engagement strategies.
    - o **Youth Organizations**: Encouraging participation through groups like the Boy Scouts, Girl Scouts, or 4-H.

Challenges and Opportunities
- **Educational Gaps**:
    - o **Resource Disparities**: Unequal access to quality civic education across different regions and populations.
    - o **Curriculum Prioritization**: Balancing civics with other academic requirements.
- **Engaging Diverse Populations**:
    - o **Inclusivity**: Ensuring civic education is relevant and accessible to all cultural and linguistic groups.
    - o **Addressing Disillusionment**: Countering apathy by demonstrating the impact of civic participation.

17.7 Respecting Diverse Perspectives and Promoting Civil Discourse

Fostering a Collaborative and Inclusive Society

In a pluralistic society, engaging with diverse viewpoints and practicing respectful communication are vital components of civic responsibility.

Importance of Civil Discourse
- **Democratic Deliberation**: Constructive dialogue enables the exchange of ideas and informed decision-making.
- **Social Cohesion**: Respectful interactions build trust and understanding among community members.
- **Conflict Resolution**: Civil discourse helps address disagreements peacefully.

Practicing Respect and Inclusivity
- **Active Listening**: Paying attention to others' perspectives without immediate judgment.
- **Empathy**: Recognizing and appreciating the experiences and feelings of others.
- **Open-Mindedness**: Being willing to consider new information and revise one's views.

Challenges to Civil Discourse
- **Polarization**:

- o **Ideological Divides**: Deep-seated differences can hinder constructive conversations.
- o **Echo Chambers**: Social media and selective media consumption reinforce existing beliefs.
- **Misinformation**:
  - o **False Narratives**: Spread of unverified or misleading information can fuel division.
  - o **Critical Evaluation**: Necessity for individuals to verify facts and sources.

Promoting Positive Engagement
- **Education and Training**:
  - o **Communication Skills**: Teaching strategies for effective dialogue and debate.
  - o **Conflict Mediation**: Providing tools to manage and resolve disputes.
- **Community Initiatives**:
  - o **Forums and Dialogues**: Creating spaces for diverse groups to discuss issues.
  - o **Collaborative Projects**: Working together on community goals fosters unity.

17.8 Advocating for Change and Social Justice

Engaging in Efforts to Improve Society

Citizens have the power and responsibility to address societal issues and advocate for policies that promote justice and equality.

Forms of Advocacy
- **Political Activism**:
  - o **Petitioning**: Gathering support to request action from government officials.
  - o **Protesting**: Peaceful demonstrations to raise awareness and demand change.
-
  - o **Lobbying**: Communicating with legislators to influence policy decisions.
- **Legal Action**:
  - o **Litigation**: Using the court system to challenge unjust laws or practices.
  - o **Amicus Briefs**: Submitting information to assist courts in understanding broader implications.
- **Grassroots Movements**:
  - o **Community Organizing**: Mobilizing local efforts to address specific issues.
  - o **Coalition Building**: Forming alliances among groups with shared goals.

Historical Examples
- **Civil Rights Movement**:
  - o **Leaders**: Figures like Dr. Martin Luther King Jr. advocated for racial equality through nonviolent means.
  - o **Outcomes**: Significant legislative changes, such as the Civil Rights Act of 1964.
- **Women's Suffrage**:
  - o **Activists**: Susan B. Anthony, Elizabeth Cady Stanton, and others fought for women's right to vote.
  - o **Achievement**: Ratification of the Nineteenth Amendment.
- **Environmental Movement**:
  - o **Advocacy**: Efforts to address pollution, conservation, and climate change.
  - o **Legislation**: Laws like the Clean Air Act and Clean Water Act.

Ethical Considerations
- **Nonviolence**: Upholding peaceful methods to effect change.
- **Legal Compliance**: Balancing civil disobedience with respect for the law.
- **Responsibility to Truth**: Ensuring advocacy is based on accurate information.

Chapter 18: The Future of Constitutional Governance

As you reach the culmination of this exploration into the United States Constitution, it is both fitting and necessary to contemplate the future of constitutional governance. The Constitution has withstood the test of time, adapting through amendments, interpretations, and societal shifts. However, the challenges and opportunities of the 21st century present new questions about how this foundational document will continue to guide the nation. This chapter delves into the potential trajectories of constitutional governance, considering technological advancements, evolving political landscapes, and the ongoing quest to realize the Constitution's ideals fully.

18.1 Technological Advancements and the Constitution

Navigating Rights and Laws in the Digital Age

The rapid pace of technological innovation has profound implications for constitutional governance. As society becomes increasingly interconnected through digital means, questions arise about how constitutional rights apply in cyberspace.

Privacy and Surveillance
- **Fourth Amendment Challenges**:
  - **Data Collection**: Government and corporate collection of personal data tests the boundaries of unreasonable searches and seizures.
  - **Warrants and Digital Information**: Courts grapple with the necessity and scope of warrants for accessing emails, cloud storage, and metadata.
- **Artificial Intelligence (AI)**:
  - **Facial Recognition**: The use of AI in surveillance raises concerns about privacy and potential biases.
  - **Predictive Policing**: AI algorithms used in law enforcement may infringe on individual rights and perpetuate discrimination.

Freedom of Expression Online
- **First Amendment Considerations**:
  - **Social Media Platforms**: Debates continue over whether platforms should be treated as public forums subject to free speech protections.
  - **Content Moderation**: Balancing the removal of harmful content with the protection of free expression.
- **Cybersecurity and National Security**:
  - **Encryption**: Tensions between privacy advocates and government agencies over access to encrypted communications.
  - **Cyber Warfare**: The need for constitutional frameworks to address state-sponsored cyber attacks and digital defense strategies.

Intellectual Property and Innovation
- **Balancing Protection and Progress**:
  - **Patent Laws**: Adapting intellectual property rights to encourage innovation while preventing monopolization.
  - **Access to Information**: Ensuring that laws do not stifle the free flow of ideas and creativity.

18.2 Demographic Shifts and Representation

Addressing Changes in Population and Diversity

The United States is experiencing significant demographic changes, including shifts in racial, ethnic, and age compositions. These changes have implications for representation and governance.

Redistricting and Gerrymandering
- **Fair Representation**:
  - **Technological Precision**: Advanced mapping tools enable more precise manipulation of electoral districts.
  - **Legal Challenges**: Courts may need to revisit standards for evaluating partisan and racial gerrymandering under the Equal Protection Clause.
- **Population Movement**:
  - **Urbanization**: The migration to urban centers affects the balance of representation between urban and rural areas.
  - **Census Accuracy**: Ensuring that population counts reflect reality is crucial for apportionment and resource allocation.

Electoral College Reforms
- **Reflecting the Popular Will**:

- Debates Over Relevance: Discussions on whether the Electoral College aligns with contemporary democratic principles.
- Alternatives:
  - National Popular Vote Interstate Compact: An agreement among states to award electoral votes to the national popular vote winner.
  - Constitutional Amendments: Proposals to abolish or modify the Electoral College structure.

Youth Engagement
- **Lowering the Voting Age**:
  - Advocacy for Inclusion: Movements to extend voting rights to 16- and 17-year-olds, recognizing their stake in future policies.
- **Civic Education**:
  - Preparing Future Citizens: Emphasizing the importance of civic knowledge and participation among younger generations.

18.3 Political Polarization and Constitutional Stability

Navigating Division and Seeking Common Ground

Increasing political polarization presents challenges to constitutional governance, testing the resilience of democratic institutions.

Erosion of Norms
- **Institutional Trust**:
  - Declining Confidence: Public trust in government branches and media is waning, affecting legitimacy.
  - Impact on Governance: Partisan gridlock can hinder the government's ability to function effectively.
- **Respect for Constitutional Processes**:
  - Challenging Electoral Outcomes: Disputes over election integrity can undermine democratic foundations.
  - Rule of Law: Ensuring that laws are applied equally and that no individual is above the law.

Promoting Bipartisanship
- **Reforms to Encourage Cooperation**:
  - Ranked-Choice Voting: A voting system that may reduce extreme partisanship by rewarding moderate candidates.
  - Open Primaries: Allowing voters of any affiliation to participate in primaries to broaden candidate appeal.
- **Civic Initiatives**:
  - Dialogue and Deliberation: Encouraging cross-partisan conversations to find common values and solutions.
  - Community Engagement: Local efforts to bridge divides and strengthen democratic practices.

18.4 The Role of the Supreme Court in Future Governance

Shaping Constitutional Interpretation in a Changing Society

The Supreme Court will continue to play a pivotal role in interpreting the Constitution amid evolving societal norms and challenges.

Judicial Philosophies and Shifts
- **Originalism vs. Living Constitutionalism**:
  - Balancing Approaches: Future justices may influence the Court's direction based on their interpretative philosophies.
- **Court Composition**:
  - Appointments: The nomination and confirmation of justices will significantly impact constitutional jurisprudence.
  - Term Limits Debate: Discussions on implementing term limits for justices to ensure regular turnover and reduce politicization.

Landmark Cases on the Horizon
- **Emerging Legal Issues**:
  - Climate Change Litigation: Cases addressing environmental protections and government responsibilities.
  - Biotechnology and Ethics: Legal questions surrounding genetic editing, cloning, and reproductive rights.

- **Digital Rights**: Defining the extent of rights in virtual spaces and with emerging technologies.

18.5 Constitutional Amendments and Reforms

Considering Changes to Address Contemporary Challenges

Amending the Constitution remains a means to enact significant structural changes, though the process is intentionally rigorous.

Potential Amendment Topics
- **Electoral Reforms**:
  - **Voting Rights Protections**: Strengthening provisions to prevent discrimination and ensure access.
  - **Campaign Finance**: Addressing the influence of money in politics through constitutional means.
- **Equal Rights Amendment (ERA)**:
  - **Gender Equality**: Renewed efforts to ratify the ERA or introduce new amendments to guarantee equal rights.
- **Term Limits for Congress**:
  - **Legislative Turnover**: Proposals to limit the number of terms for senators and representatives to promote fresh perspectives.

Challenges in Amendment Process
- **Political Polarization**: Achieving the required consensus is more difficult in a divided political climate.
- **Alternative Avenues**:
  - **Legislative Actions**: Passing laws to address issues without constitutional amendments.
  - **Judicial Interpretation**: Courts adapting constitutional principles to contemporary contexts.

18.6 Globalization and International Influence

The Constitution in a Connected World

Global interconnectedness affects constitutional governance, as international events and norms influence domestic policies.

International Law and Agreements
- **Treaty Obligations**:
  - **Supremacy Clause**: The Constitution establishes treaties as the supreme law of the land, raising questions about sovereignty and compliance.
- **Human Rights Commitments**:
  - **Global Standards**: Balancing international human rights obligations with constitutional interpretations.

Cybersecurity and International Cooperation
- **Cross-Border Challenges**:
  - **Cyber Threats**: Collaborative efforts needed to address cybercrime and digital security.
- **Regulatory Harmonization**:
  - **Data Protection**: Aligning privacy laws with international frameworks like the GDPR.

Migration and Refugee Policies
- **Constitutional Protections**:
  - **Due Process**: Ensuring fair treatment of immigrants and asylum seekers under constitutional principles.
- **Global Responsibility**:
  - **International Collaboration**: Working with other nations to address root causes of migration and uphold human rights.

18.7 Environmental Challenges and Constitutional Rights

Addressing Climate Change and Environmental Protection

Environmental issues pose significant challenges that intersect with constitutional governance.

Environmental Rights
- **Constitutional Amendments**:
  - **Right to a Healthy Environment**: Movements advocating for explicit constitutional recognition of environmental rights.
- **Legal Precedents**:
  - **Public Trust Doctrine**: Courts interpreting government obligations to protect natural resources for public use.

Governmental Responsibilities
- **Regulatory Authority**:
  - **Commerce Clause**: Utilizing federal powers to enact environmental regulations.

- **Intergenerational Justice**:
  - **Future Generations**: Considering the rights and interests of future citizens in policy-making.

18.8 Education and Civic Engagement
Preparing Citizens for Active Participation in Governance

Strengthening constitutional governance requires an informed and engaged populace.

Civic Education
- **Curriculum Development**:
  - **Emphasizing Civics**: Integrating comprehensive civic education in schools to foster understanding of governmental structures and responsibilities.
- **Critical Thinking Skills**:
  - **Media Literacy**: Teaching individuals to assess information critically to combat misinformation.

Public Participation
- **Innovative Engagement**:
  - **Digital Platforms**: Leveraging technology to facilitate public input and participation in governance.
- **Community Initiatives**:
  - **Local Governance**: Encouraging involvement in municipal decisions to strengthen democratic practices at the grassroots level.

18.9 Preserving Democratic Ideals
Upholding the Constitution's Principles Amidst Change

As the nation faces future challenges, the core principles of the Constitution remain a guiding force.

Rule of Law
- **Equal Application**: Ensuring laws are applied fairly and justice is accessible to all.
- **Judicial Independence**: Protecting the judiciary from undue influence to maintain impartiality.

Protection of Rights
- **Minority Rights**: Safeguarding the rights of all individuals, especially marginalized groups.
- **Adaptation of Rights**: Interpreting constitutional protections to remain relevant in new contexts.

Checks and Balances
- **Institutional Integrity**: Maintaining the separation of powers to prevent the concentration of authority.
- **Oversight Mechanisms**: Strengthening transparency and accountability in government actions.

Appendix A: Full Text of the Declaration of Independence

The **Declaration of Independence** is one of the most significant documents in American history. Adopted by the **Second Continental Congress** on **July 4, 1776**, it announced the thirteen American colonies' separation from British rule and articulated the fundamental principles of individual liberty and government by consent. Drafted primarily by **Thomas Jefferson**, the Declaration eloquently outlines the colonies' grievances against King George III and asserts the inherent rights of all people.

IN CONGRESS, JULY 4, 1776

The unanimous Declaration of the thirteen united States of America

When in the Course of human events it becomes necessary for one people to dissolve the political bands which have connected them with another, and to assume among the Powers of the Earth, the separate and equal Station to which the Laws of Nature and of Nature's God entitle them, a decent Respect to the Opinions of Mankind requires that they should declare the causes which impel them to the Separation.

We hold these Truths to be self-evident, that all Men are created equal, that they are endowed by their Creator with certain unalienable Rights, that among these are Life, Liberty, and the Pursuit of Happiness.—That to secure these Rights, Governments are instituted among Men, deriving their just Powers from the Consent of the Governed,—That whenever any Form of Government becomes destructive of these Ends, it is the Right of the People to alter or to abolish it, and to institute new Government, laying its Foundation on such Principles, and organizing its Powers in such Form, as to them shall seem most likely to effect their Safety and Happiness. Prudence, indeed, will dictate that Governments long established should not be changed for light and transient Causes; and accordingly all Experience hath shown, that Mankind are more disposed to suffer, while Evils are sufferable, than to right themselves by abolishing the Forms to which they are accustomed. **But when a long Train of Abuses and Usurpations, pursuing invariably the same Object evinces a Design to reduce them under absolute Despotism,** it is their Right, it is their Duty, to throw off such Government, and to provide new Guards for their future Security.—Such has been the patient Sufferance of these Colonies; and such is now the Necessity which constrains them to alter their former Systems of Government. **The History of the present King of Great Britain is a History of repeated Injuries and Usurpations, all having in direct Object the Establishment of an absolute Tyranny over these States.** To prove this, let Facts be submitted to a candid World.

- He has refused his Assent to Laws, the most wholesome and necessary for the public Good.

- He has forbidden his Governors to pass Laws of immediate and pressing Importance, unless suspended in their Operation till his Assent should be obtained; and when so suspended, he has utterly neglected to attend to them.

- He has refused to pass other Laws for the Accommodation of large Districts of People, unless those People would relinquish the Right of Representation in the Legislature, a Right inestimable to them and formidable to Tyrants only.

- He has called together legislative Bodies at Places unusual, uncomfortable, and distant from the Depository of their public Records, for the sole Purpose of fatiguing them into Compliance with his Measures.

- He has dissolved Representative Houses repeatedly, for opposing with manly Firmness his Invasions on the Rights of the People.

- He has refused for a long Time, after such Dissolutions, to cause others to be elected; whereby the Legislative Powers, incapable of Annihilation, have returned to the People at large for their exercise; the State remaining, in the meantime, exposed to all the Dangers of Invasion from without, and Convulsions within.

- He has endeavored to prevent the Population of these States; for that Purpose obstructing the Laws for Naturalization of Foreigners; refusing to pass others to encourage their Migrations hither, and raising the Conditions of new Appropriations of Lands.

- He has obstructed the Administration of Justice, by refusing his Assent to Laws for establishing Judiciary Powers.

- He has made Judges dependent on his Will alone, for the Tenure of their Offices, and the Amount and Payment of their Salaries.

- He has erected a multitude of New Offices, and sent hither Swarms of Officers to harass our People, and eat out their Substance.

- He has kept among us, in Times of Peace, Standing Armies without the Consent of our Legislatures.

- He has affected to render the Military independent of and superior to the Civil Power.

- He has combined with others to subject us to a Jurisdiction foreign to our Constitution, and unacknowledged by our Laws; giving his Assent to their Acts of pretended Legislation:
    - For Quartering large Bodies of Armed Troops among us:
    - For protecting them, by a mock Trial, from Punishment for any Murders which they should commit on the Inhabitants of these States:
    - For cutting off our Trade with all Parts of the World:
    - For imposing Taxes on us without our Consent:
    - For depriving us, in many Cases, of the Benefits of Trial by Jury:
    - For transporting us beyond Seas to be tried for pretended Offenses:
    - For abolishing the free System of English Laws in a neighboring Province, establishing therein an Arbitrary Government, and enlarging its Boundaries, so as to render it at once an Example and fit Instrument for introducing the same absolute Rule into these Colonies:
    - For taking away our Charters, abolishing our most valuable Laws, and altering fundamentally the Forms of our Governments:
    - For suspending our own Legislatures, and declaring themselves invested with Power to legislate for us in all Cases whatsoever.

He has abdicated Government here, by declaring us out of his Protection and waging War against us.

- He has plundered our Seas, ravaged our Coasts, burned our Towns, and destroyed the Lives of our People.

- He is at this time transporting large Armies of foreign Mercenaries to complete the Works of Death, Desolation, and Tyranny, already begun with circumstances of Cruelty and perfidy scarcely paralleled in the most barbarous Ages, and totally unworthy the Head of a civilized Nation.

- He has constrained our fellow Citizens taken Captive on the high Seas to bear Arms against their Country, to become the Executioners of their Friends and Brethren, or to fall themselves by their Hands.

- He has excited domestic Insurrections amongst us, and has endeavored to bring on the Inhabitants of our Frontiers, the merciless Indian Savages, whose known Rule of Warfare is an undistinguished Destruction of all Ages, Sexes, and Conditions.

In every stage of these Oppressions we have Petitioned for Redress in the most humble Terms: Our repeated Petitions have been answered only by repeated Injury. A Prince whose character is thus marked by every act which may define a Tyrant, is unfit to be the ruler of a free people.

Nor have we been wanting in Attentions to our British brethren. We have warned them from time to time of attempts by their legislature to extend an unwarrantable jurisdiction over us. **We have reminded them of the circumstances of our emigration and settlement here.** We have appealed to their native justice and magnanimity, and we have conjured them by the ties of our common kindred to disavow these usurpations, which would inevitably interrupt our connections and correspondence. **They too have been deaf to the voice of justice and of consanguinity.** We must, therefore, acquiesce in the necessity, which denounces our Separation, and hold them, as we hold the rest of mankind, Enemies in War, in Peace Friends.

We, therefore, the Representatives of the united States of America, in General Congress, Assembled, appealing to the Supreme Judge of the World for the rectitude of our intentions, do, in the Name, and by Authority of the good People of these Colonies, solemnly publish and declare, **That these United Colonies are, and of Right ought to be Free and Independent States;** that they are Absolved from all Allegiance to the British Crown, and that all political connection between them and the State of Great Britain is and ought to be totally dissolved; **and that as Free and Independent States, they have full Power to levy War, conclude Peace, contract Alliances, establish Commerce, and to do all other Acts and Things which Independent States may of right do.** And for the support of this Declaration, with a firm reliance on the Protection of divine Providence, **we mutually pledge to each other our Lives, our Fortunes, and our sacred Honor.**

Signatories

Georgia

- Button Gwinnett
- Lyman Hall
- George Walton

North Carolina

- William Hooper
- Joseph Hewes
- John Penn

South Carolina

- Edward Rutledge
- Thomas Heyward, Jr.
- Thomas Lynch, Jr.
- Arthur Middleton

Massachusetts

- John Hancock

Maryland

- Samuel Chase
- William Paca
- Thomas Stone
- Charles Carroll of Carrollton

Virginia
- George Wythe
- Richard Henry Lee
- Thomas Jefferson
- Benjamin Harrison
- Thomas Nelson, Jr.
- Francis Lightfoot Lee
- Carter Braxton

Pennsylvania
- Robert Morris
- Benjamin Rush
- Benjamin Franklin
- John Morton
- George Clymer
- James Smith
- George Taylor
- James Wilson
- George Ross

Delaware
- Caesar Rodney
- George Read
- Thomas McKean

New York
- William Floyd
- Philip Livingston
- Francis Lewis
- Lewis Morris

New Jersey

- Richard Stockton
- John Witherspoon
- Francis Hopkinson
- John Hart
- Abraham Clark

New Hampshire

- Josiah Bartlett
- William Whipple
- Matthew Thornton

Rhode Island

- Stephen Hopkins
- William Ellery

Connecticut

- Roger Sherman
- Samuel Huntington
- William Williams
- Oliver Wolcott

Massachusetts Bay

- Samuel Adams
- John Adams
- Robert Treat Paine
- Elbridge Gerry

Appendix B: Full Text of the United States Constitution

The **United States Constitution** is the supreme law of the United States of America. Drafted during the Constitutional Convention in Philadelphia in 1787 and ratified by the required number of states in 1788, it replaced the Articles of Confederation and established the framework for the federal government. The Constitution delineates the structure of the government, enumerates the powers of its three branches, and protects the rights of citizens through its amendments, including the Bill of Rights.

Preamble

"We the People of the United States, in Order to form a more perfect Union, establish Justice, insure domestic Tranquility, provide for the common defence, promote the general Welfare, and secure the Blessings of Liberty to ourselves and our Posterity, do ordain and establish this Constitution for the United States of America."

Article I

Section 1

All legislative Powers herein granted shall be vested in a Congress of the United States, which shall consist of a Senate and House of Representatives.

Section 2

1. The House of Representatives shall be composed of Members chosen every second Year by the People of the several States, and the Electors in each State shall have the Qualifications requisite for Electors of the most numerous Branch of the State Legislature.

2. No Person shall be a Representative who shall not have attained to the Age of twenty-five Years, and been seven Years a Citizen of the United States, and who shall not, when elected, be an Inhabitant of that State in which he shall be chosen.

3. Representatives and direct Taxes shall be apportioned among the several States which may be included within this Union, according to their respective Numbers, which shall be determined by adding to the whole Number of free Persons, including those bound to Service for a Term of Years, and excluding Indians not taxed, three-fifths of all other Persons. *(Note: This clause was modified by the Fourteenth Amendment.)* The actual Enumeration shall be made within three Years after the first Meeting of the Congress of the United States, and within every subsequent Term of ten Years, in such Manner as they shall by Law direct. The Number of Representatives shall not exceed one for every thirty Thousand, but each State shall have at least one Representative; and until such Enumeration shall be made, the State of New Hampshire shall be entitled to choose three, Massachusetts eight, Rhode Island and Providence Plantations one, Connecticut five, New York six, New Jersey four, Pennsylvania eight, Delaware one, Maryland six, Virginia ten, North Carolina five, South Carolina five, and Georgia three.

4. When vacancies happen in the Representation from any State, the Executive Authority thereof shall issue Writs of Election to fill such Vacancies.

5. The House of Representatives shall choose their Speaker and other Officers; and shall have the sole Power of Impeachment.

Section 3

1. The Senate of the United States shall be composed of two Senators from each State, chosen by the Legislature thereof, for six Years; and each Senator shall have one Vote. *(Note: The Seventeenth Amendment changed the method of selecting Senators to direct election by the people.)*

2. Immediately after they shall be assembled in Consequence of the first Election, they shall be divided as equally as may be into three Classes. The Seats of the Senators of the first Class shall be vacated at the Expiration of the second Year, of the second Class at the Expiration of the fourth Year, and of the third Class at the Expiration of the sixth Year, so that one-third may be chosen every second Year; and if Vacancies happen by Resignation, or otherwise, during the Recess of the Legislature of any State, the Executive thereof may make temporary Appointments until the next Meeting of the Legislature, which shall then fill such Vacancies.

3. No Person shall be a Senator who shall not have attained to the Age of thirty Years, and been nine Years a Citizen of the United States, and who shall not, when elected, be an Inhabitant of that State for which he shall be chosen.

4. The Vice President of the United States shall be President of the Senate, but shall have no Vote, unless they be equally divided.

5. The Senate shall choose their other Officers, and also a President pro tempore, in the Absence of the Vice President, or when he shall exercise the Office of President of the United States.

6. The Senate shall have the sole Power to try all Impeachments. When sitting for that Purpose, they shall be on Oath or Affirmation. When the President of the United States is tried, the Chief Justice shall preside: And no Person shall be convicted without the Concurrence of two-thirds of the Members present.

7. Judgment in Cases of Impeachment shall not extend further than to removal from Office, and disqualification to hold and enjoy any Office of honor, Trust or Profit under the United States: but the Party convicted shall nevertheless be liable and subject to Indictment, Trial, Judgment and Punishment, according to Law.

Section 4

1. The Times, Places and Manner of holding Elections for Senators and Representatives, shall be prescribed in each State by the Legislature thereof; but the Congress may at any time by Law make or alter such Regulations, except as to the Places of choosing Senators.

2. The Congress shall assemble at least once in every Year, and such Meeting shall be on the first Monday in December, unless they shall by Law appoint a different Day.

Section 5

1. Each House shall be the Judge of the Elections, Returns and Qualifications of its own Members, and a Majority of each shall constitute a Quorum to do Business; but a smaller Number may adjourn from day to day, and may be authorized to compel the Attendance of absent Members, in such Manner, and under such Penalties as each House may provide.

2. Each House may determine the Rules of its Proceedings, punish its Members for disorderly Behavior, and, with the Concurrence of two-thirds, expel a Member.

3. Each House shall keep a Journal of its Proceedings, and from time to time publish the same, excepting such Parts as may in their Judgment require Secrecy; and the Yeas and Nays of the Members of either House on any question shall, at the Desire of one-fifth of those Present, be entered on the Journal.

4. Neither House, during the Session of Congress, shall, without the Consent of the other, adjourn for more than three days, nor to any other Place than that in which the two Houses shall be sitting.

Section 6

1. The Senators and Representatives shall receive a Compensation for their Services, to be ascertained by Law, and paid out of the Treasury of the United States. They shall in all Cases, except Treason, Felony and Breach of the Peace, be privileged from Arrest during their Attendance at the Session of their respective Houses, and in going to and returning from the same; and for any Speech or Debate in either House, they shall not be questioned in any other Place.

2. No Senator or Representative shall, during the Time for which he was elected, be appointed to any civil Office under the Authority of the United States which shall have been created, or the Emoluments whereof shall have been increased during such time; and no Person holding any Office under the United States shall be a Member of either House during his Continuance in Office.

Section 7

1. All Bills for raising Revenue shall originate in the House of Representatives; but the Senate may propose or concur with Amendments as on other Bills.

2. Every Bill which shall have passed the House of Representatives and the Senate shall, before it becomes a Law, be presented to the President of the United States; If he approve he shall sign it, but if not he shall return it, with his Objections, to that House in which it shall have originated, who shall enter the Objections at large on their Journal, and proceed to reconsider it. If after such Reconsideration two-thirds of that House shall agree to pass the Bill, it shall be sent, together with the Objections, to the other House, by which it shall likewise be reconsidered, and if approved by two-thirds of that House, it shall become a Law. But in all such Cases the Votes of both Houses shall be determined by Yeas and Nays, and the Names of the Persons voting for and against the Bill shall be entered on the Journal of each House respectively. If any Bill shall not be returned by the President within ten Days (Sundays excepted) after it shall have been presented to him, the Same shall be a Law, in like Manner as if he had signed it, unless the Congress by their Adjournment prevent its Return, in which Case it shall not be a Law.

3. Every Order, Resolution, or Vote to which the Concurrence of the Senate and House of Representatives may be necessary (except on a question of Adjournment) shall be presented to the President of the United States; and before the Same shall take Effect, shall be approved by him, or being disapproved by him, shall be repassed by two-thirds of the Senate and House of Representatives, according to the Rules and Limitations prescribed in the Case of a Bill.

Section 8

The Congress shall have Power:

1. To lay and collect Taxes, Duties, Imposts and Excises, to pay the Debts and provide for the common Defence and general Welfare of the United States; but all Duties, Imposts and Excises shall be uniform throughout the United States;

2. To borrow Money on the credit of the United States;

3. To regulate Commerce with foreign Nations, and among the several States, and with the Indian Tribes;

4. To establish an uniform Rule of Naturalization, and uniform Laws on the subject of Bankruptcies throughout the United States;

5. To coin Money, regulate the Value thereof, and of foreign Coin, and fix the Standard of Weights and Measures;

6. To provide for the Punishment of counterfeiting the Securities and current Coin of the United States;

7. To establish Post Offices and post Roads;

8. To promote the Progress of Science and useful Arts, by securing for limited Times to Authors and Inventors the exclusive Right to their respective Writings and Discoveries;

9. To constitute Tribunals inferior to the Supreme Court;

10. To define and punish Piracies and Felonies committed on the high Seas, and Offences against the Law of Nations;

11. To declare War, grant Letters of Marque and Reprisal, and make Rules concerning Captures on Land and Water;

12. To raise and support Armies, but no Appropriation of Money to that Use shall be for a longer Term than two Years;

13. To provide and maintain a Navy;

14. To make Rules for the Government and Regulation of the land and naval Forces;

15. To provide for calling forth the Militia to execute the Laws of the Union, suppress Insurrections and repel Invasions;

16. To provide for organizing, arming, and disciplining, the Militia, and for governing such Part of them as may be employed in the Service of the United States, reserving to the States respectively, the Appointment of the Officers, and the Authority of training the Militia according to the discipline prescribed by Congress;

17. To exercise exclusive Legislation in all Cases whatsoever, over such District (not exceeding ten Miles square) as may, by Cession of particular States, and the Acceptance of Congress, become the Seat of the Government of the United States, and to exercise like Authority over all Places purchased by the Consent of the Legislature of the State in which the Same shall be, for the Erection of Forts, Magazines, Arsenals, Dock-Yards, and other needful Buildings;—And

18. To make all Laws which shall be necessary and proper for carrying into Execution the foregoing Powers, and all other Powers vested by this Constitution in the Government of the United States or in any Department or Officer thereof.

Section 9

1. The Migration or Importation of such Persons as any of the States now existing shall think proper to admit, shall not be prohibited by the Congress prior to the Year one thousand eight hundred and eight, but a Tax or duty may be imposed on such Importation, not exceeding ten dollars for each Person.

2. The Privilege of the Writ of Habeas Corpus shall not be suspended, unless when in Cases of Rebellion or Invasion the public Safety may require it.

3. No Bill of Attainder or ex post facto Law shall be passed.

4. No Capitation, or other direct, Tax shall be laid, unless in Proportion to the Census or Enumeration herein before directed to be taken. *(Note: Modified by the Sixteenth Amendment.)*

5. No Tax or Duty shall be laid on Articles exported from any State.

6. No Preference shall be given by any Regulation of Commerce or Revenue to the Ports of one State over those of another; nor shall Vessels bound to, or from, one State, be obliged to enter, clear, or pay Duties in another.

7. No Money shall be drawn from the Treasury, but in Consequence of Appropriations made by Law; and a regular Statement and Account of the Receipts and Expenditures of all public Money shall be published from time to time.

8. No Title of Nobility shall be granted by the United States: And no Person holding any Office of Profit or Trust under them, shall, without the Consent of the Congress, accept of any present, Emolument, Office, or Title, of any kind whatever, from any King, Prince, or foreign State.

Section 10

1. No State shall enter into any Treaty, Alliance, or Confederation; grant Letters of Marque and Reprisal; coin Money; emit Bills of Credit; make any Thing but gold and silver Coin a Tender in Payment of Debts; pass any Bill of Attainder, ex post facto Law, or Law impairing the Obligation of Contracts, or grant any Title of Nobility.

2. No State shall, without the Consent of the Congress, lay any Imposts or Duties on Imports or Exports, except what may be absolutely necessary for executing its inspection Laws: and the net Produce of all Duties and Imposts, laid by any State on Imports or Exports, shall be for the Use of the Treasury of the United States; and all such Laws shall be subject to the Revision and Controul of the Congress.

3. No State shall, without the Consent of Congress, lay any Duty of Tonnage, keep Troops, or Ships of War in time of Peace, enter into any Agreement or Compact with another State, or with a foreign Power, or engage in War, unless actually invaded, or in such imminent Danger as will not admit of delay.

Article II

Section 1

1. The executive Power shall be vested in a President of the United States of America. He shall hold his Office during the Term of four Years, and, together with the Vice President chosen for the same Term, be elected as follows:

2. Each State shall appoint, in such Manner as the Legislature thereof may direct, a Number of Electors equal to the whole Number of Senators and Representatives to which the State may be entitled in the Congress: but no Senator or Representative, or Person holding an Office of Trust or Profit under the United States, shall be appointed an Elector.

3. *(Note: This clause was superseded by the Twelfth Amendment.)* The Electors shall meet in their respective States, and vote by Ballot for two Persons, of whom one at least shall not be an Inhabitant of the same State with themselves. And they shall make a List of all the Persons voted for, and of the Number of Votes for each; which List they shall sign and certify, and transmit sealed to the Seat of the Government of the United States, directed to the President of the Senate. The President of the Senate shall, in the Presence of the Senate and House of Representatives, open all the Certificates, and the Votes shall then be counted. The Person having the greatest Number of Votes shall be the President, if such Number be a Majority of the whole Number of Electors appointed; and if there be more than one who have such Majority, and have an equal Number of Votes, then the House of Representatives shall immediately choose by Ballot one of them for President; and if no Person have a Majority, then from the five highest on the List the said House shall in like Manner choose the President. But in choosing the President, the Votes shall be taken by States, the Representation from each State having one Vote; a quorum for this Purpose shall consist of a Member or Members from two-thirds of the States, and a Majority of all the States shall be necessary to a Choice. In every Case, after the Choice of the President, the Person having the greatest Number of Votes of the Electors shall be the Vice President.

4. The Congress may determine the Time of choosing the Electors, and the Day on which they shall give their Votes; which Day shall be the same throughout the United States.

5. No Person except a natural born Citizen, or a Citizen of the United States, at the time of the Adoption of this Constitution, shall be eligible to the Office of President; neither shall any Person be eligible to that Office who shall not have attained to the Age of thirty-five Years, and been fourteen Years a Resident within the United States.

6. In Case of the Removal of the President from Office, or of his Death, Resignation, or Inability to discharge the Powers and Duties of the said Office, the Same shall devolve on the Vice President, and the Congress may by Law provide for the Case of Removal, Death, Resignation or Inability, both of the President and Vice President, declaring what Officer shall then act as President, and such Officer shall act accordingly, until the Disability be removed, or a President shall be elected. *(Note: Modified by the Twenty-Fifth Amendment.)*

7. The President shall, at stated Times, receive for his Services, a Compensation, which shall neither be increased nor diminished during the Period for which he shall have been elected, and he shall not receive within that Period any other Emolument from the United States, or any of them.

8. Before he enter on the Execution of his Office, he shall take the following Oath or Affirmation:—*"I do solemnly swear (or affirm) that I will faithfully execute the Office of President of the United States, and will to the best of my Ability, preserve, protect and defend the Constitution of the United States."*

Section 2

1. The President shall be Commander in Chief of the Army and Navy of the United States, and of the Militia of the several States, when called into the actual Service of the United States; he may require the Opinion, in writing, of the principal Officer in each of the executive Departments, upon any Subject relating to the Duties of their respective Offices, and he shall have Power to grant Reprieves and Pardons for Offenses against the United States, except in Cases of Impeachment.

2. He shall have Power, by and with the Advice and Consent of the Senate, to make Treaties, provided two-thirds of the Senators present concur; and he shall nominate, and by and with the Advice and Consent of the Senate, shall appoint Ambassadors, other public Ministers and Consuls, Judges of the supreme Court, and all other Officers of the United States, whose Appointments are not herein otherwise provided for, and which shall be established by Law: but the Congress may by Law vest the Appointment of such inferior Officers, as they think proper, in the President alone, in the Courts of Law, or in the Heads of Departments.

3. The President shall have Power to fill up all Vacancies that may happen during the Recess of the Senate, by granting Commissions which shall expire at the End of their next Session.

Section 3

He shall from time to time give to the Congress Information on the State of the Union, and recommend to their Consideration such Measures as he shall judge necessary and expedient; he may, on extraordinary Occasions, convene both Houses, or either of them, and in Case of Disagreement between them, with Respect to the Time of Adjournment, he may adjourn them to such Time as he shall think proper; he shall receive Ambassadors and other public Ministers; he shall take Care that the Laws be faithfully executed, and shall Commission all the Officers of the United States.

Section 4

The President, Vice President, and all civil Officers of the United States, shall be removed from Office on Impeachment for, and Conviction of, Treason, Bribery, or other high Crimes and Misdemeanors.

Article III

Section 1

The judicial Power of the United States shall be vested in one supreme Court, and in such inferior Courts as the Congress may from time to time ordain and establish. The Judges, both of the supreme and inferior Courts, shall hold their Offices during good Behavior, and shall, at stated Times, receive for their Services a Compensation which shall not be diminished during their Continuance in Office.

Section 2

1. The judicial Power shall extend to all Cases, in Law and Equity, arising under this Constitution, the Laws of the United States, and Treaties made, or which shall be made, under their Authority;—to all Cases affecting Ambassadors, other public Ministers and Consuls;—to all Cases of admiralty and maritime Jurisdiction;—to Controversies to which the United States shall be a Party;—to Controversies between two or more States;—between a State and Citizens of another State; *(Note: Modified by the Eleventh Amendment.)*—between Citizens of different States;—between Citizens of the same State claiming Lands under Grants of different States, and between a State, or the Citizens thereof, and foreign States, Citizens or Subjects.

2. In all Cases affecting Ambassadors, other public Ministers and Consuls, and those in which a State shall be Party, the supreme Court shall have original Jurisdiction. In all the other Cases before mentioned, the supreme Court shall have appellate Jurisdiction, both as to Law and Fact, with such Exceptions, and under such Regulations as the Congress shall make.

3. The Trial of all Crimes, except in Cases of Impeachment, shall be by Jury; and such Trial shall be held in the State where the said Crimes shall have been committed; but when not committed within any State, the Trial shall be at such Place or Places as the Congress may by Law have directed.

Section 3

1. Treason against the United States shall consist only in levying War against them, or in adhering to their Enemies, giving them Aid and Comfort. No Person shall be convicted of Treason unless on the Testimony of two Witnesses to the same overt Act, or on Confession in open Court.

2. The Congress shall have Power to declare the Punishment of Treason, but no Attainder of Treason shall work Corruption of Blood, or Forfeiture except during the Life of the Person attainted.

Article IV

Section 1

Full Faith and Credit shall be given in each State to the public Acts, Records, and judicial Proceedings of every other State. And the Congress may by general Laws prescribe the Manner in which such Acts, Records and Proceedings shall be proved, and the Effect thereof.

Section 2

1. The Citizens of each State shall be entitled to all Privileges and Immunities of Citizens in the several States.

2. A Person charged in any State with Treason, Felony, or other Crime, who shall flee from Justice, and be found in another State, shall on Demand of the executive Authority of the State from which he fled, be delivered up, to be removed to the State having Jurisdiction of the Crime.

3. *(Note: This clause was superseded by the Thirteenth Amendment.)* No Person held to Service or Labour in one State, under the Laws thereof, escaping into another, shall, in consequence of any Law or

Regulation therein, be discharged from such Service or Labour, but shall be delivered up on Claim of the Party to whom such Service or Labour may be due.

Section 3

1. New States may be admitted by the Congress into this Union; but no new State shall be formed or erected within the Jurisdiction of any other State; nor any State be formed by the Junction of two or more States or parts of States, without the Consent of the Legislatures of the States concerned as well as of the Congress.

2. The Congress shall have Power to dispose of and make all needful Rules and Regulations respecting the Territory or other Property belonging to the United States; and nothing in this Constitution shall be so construed as to Prejudice any Claims of the United States, or of any particular State.

Section 4

The United States shall guarantee to every State in this Union a Republican Form of Government, and shall protect each of them against Invasion; and on Application of the Legislature, or of the Executive (when the Legislature cannot be convened), against domestic Violence.

Article V

The Congress, whenever two thirds of both Houses shall deem it necessary, shall propose Amendments to this Constitution, or, on the Application of the Legislatures of two thirds of the several States, shall call a Convention for proposing Amendments, which, in either Case, shall be valid to all Intents and Purposes, as part of this Constitution, when ratified by the Legislatures of three fourths of the several States or by Conventions in three fourths thereof, as the one or the other Mode of Ratification may be proposed by the Congress; **Provided** that no Amendment which may be made prior to the Year One thousand eight hundred and eight shall in any Manner affect the first and fourth Clauses in the Ninth Section of the first Article; **and that no State, without its Consent, shall be deprived of its equal Suffrage in the Senate.**

Article VI

1. All Debts contracted and Engagements entered into, before the Adoption of this Constitution, shall be as valid against the United States under this Constitution, as under the Confederation.

2. This Constitution, and the Laws of the United States which shall be made in Pursuance thereof; and all Treaties made, or which shall be made, under the Authority of the United States, **shall be the supreme Law of the Land**; and the Judges in every State shall be bound thereby, anything in the Constitution or Laws of any State to the Contrary notwithstanding.

3. The Senators and Representatives before mentioned, and the Members of the several State Legislatures, and all executive and judicial Officers, both of the United States and of the several States, **shall be bound by Oath or Affirmation, to support this Constitution**; but no religious Test shall ever be required as a Qualification to any Office or public Trust under the United States.

Article VII

The Ratification of the Conventions of nine States, shall be sufficient for the Establishment of this Constitution between the States so ratifying the Same.

Attestation

Done in Convention by the Unanimous Consent of the States present the Seventeenth Day of September in the Year of our Lord one thousand seven hundred and eighty-seven and of the Independence of the United States of America the Twelfth.

In Witness whereof We have hereunto subscribed our Names,

George Washington President and deputy from Virginia

[Followed by the signatures of the delegates from the twelve states present.]

Amendments to the United States Constitution

The United States Constitution has been amended 27 times since its ratification in 1788. These amendments address various aspects of governance, rights, and liberties, reflecting the evolving values and challenges of the nation. Below is the full text of each amendment.

Amendment I (1791)

Freedom of Religion, Speech, Press, Assembly, and Petition

"Congress shall make no law respecting an establishment of religion, or prohibiting the free exercise thereof; or abridging the freedom of speech, or of the press; or the right of the people peaceably to assemble, and to petition the Government for a redress of grievances."

Amendment II (1791)

Right to Keep and Bear Arms

"A well regulated Militia, being necessary to the security of a free State, the right of the people to keep and bear Arms, shall not be infringed."

Amendment III (1791)

Quartering of Soldiers

"No Soldier shall, in time of peace be quartered in any house, without the consent of the Owner, nor in time of war, but in a manner to be prescribed by law."

Amendment IV (1791)

Search and Seizure

"The right of the people to be secure in their persons, houses, papers, and effects, against unreasonable searches and seizures, shall not be violated, and no Warrants shall issue, but upon probable cause, supported by Oath or affirmation, and particularly describing the place to be searched, and the persons or things to be seized."

Amendment V (1791)

Rights in Criminal Cases

"No person shall be held to answer for a capital, or otherwise infamous crime, unless on a presentment or indictment of a Grand Jury, except in cases arising in the land or naval forces, or in the Militia, when in actual service in time of War or public danger; nor shall any person be subject for the same offence to be twice put in jeopardy of life or limb; nor shall be compelled in any criminal case to be a witness against himself, nor be deprived of life, liberty, or property, without due process of law; nor shall private property be taken for public use, without just compensation."

Amendment VI (1791)

Right to a Fair Trial

"In all criminal prosecutions, the accused shall enjoy the right to a speedy and public trial, by an impartial jury of the State and district wherein the crime shall have been committed, which district shall have been previously ascertained by law, and to be informed of the nature and cause of the accusation; to be confronted with the

witnesses against him; to have compulsory process for obtaining witnesses in his favor, and to have the Assistance of Counsel for his defence."

Amendment VII (1791)

Rights in Civil Cases

"In Suits at common law, where the value in controversy shall exceed twenty dollars, the right of trial by jury shall be preserved, and no fact tried by a jury, shall be otherwise re-examined in any Court of the United States, than according to the rules of the common law."

Amendment VIII (1791)

Bail, Fines, and Punishments

"Excessive bail shall not be required, nor excessive fines imposed, nor cruel and unusual punishments inflicted."

Amendment IX (1791)

Rights Retained by the People

"The enumeration in the Constitution, of certain rights, shall not be construed to deny or disparage others retained by the people."

Amendment X (1791)

States' Rights

"The powers not delegated to the United States by the Constitution, nor prohibited by it to the States, are reserved to the States respectively, or to the people."

Amendment XI (1795)

Lawsuits Against States

"The Judicial power of the United States shall not be construed to extend to any suit in law or equity, commenced or prosecuted against one of the United States by Citizens of another State, or by Citizens or Subjects of any Foreign State."

Amendment XII (1804)

Election of President and Vice President

"The Electors shall meet in their respective states and vote by ballot for President and Vice-President, one of whom, at least, shall not be an inhabitant of the same state with themselves; they shall name in their ballots the person voted for as President, and in distinct ballots the person voted for as Vice-President, and they shall make distinct lists of all persons voted for as President, and of all persons voted for as Vice-President, and of the number of votes for each, which lists they shall sign and certify, and transmit sealed to the seat of the government of the United States, directed to the President of the Senate;—The President of the Senate shall, in the presence of the Senate and House of Representatives, open all the certificates and the votes shall then be counted;—The person having the greatest number of votes for President, shall be the President, if such number be a majority of the whole number of Electors appointed; and if no person have such majority, then from the persons having the highest numbers not exceeding three on the list of those voted for as President, the House of Representatives shall choose immediately, by ballot, the President. But in choosing the President, the votes shall be taken by states, the representation from each state having one vote; a quorum for this purpose shall consist of a member or members from two-thirds of the states, and a majority of all the states shall be necessary to a choice. And if the House of Representatives shall not choose a President whenever the right of choice shall devolve upon them, before the fourth day of March next following, then the Vice-President shall act as President, as in the case of the

death or other constitutional disability of the President.—The person having the greatest number of votes as Vice-President, shall be the Vice-President, if such number be a majority of the whole number of Electors appointed, and if no person have a majority, then from the two highest numbers on the list, the Senate shall choose the Vice-President; a quorum for the purpose shall consist of two-thirds of the whole number of Senators, and a majority of the whole number shall be necessary to a choice. But no person constitutionally ineligible to the office of President shall be eligible to that of Vice-President of the United States."

Amendment XIII (1865)

Abolition of Slavery

Section 1.

"Neither slavery nor involuntary servitude, except as a punishment for crime whereof the party shall have been duly convicted, shall exist within the United States, or any place subject to their jurisdiction."

Section 2.

"Congress shall have power to enforce this article by appropriate legislation."

Amendment XIV (1868)

Citizenship, Due Process, and Equal Protection

Section 1.

"All persons born or naturalized in the United States, and subject to the jurisdiction thereof, are citizens of the United States and of the State wherein they reside. No State shall make or enforce any law which shall abridge the privileges or immunities of citizens of the United States; nor shall any State deprive any person of life, liberty, or property, without due process of law; nor deny to any person within its jurisdiction the equal protection of the laws."

Section 2.

"Representatives shall be apportioned among the several States according to their respective numbers, counting the whole number of persons in each State, excluding Indians not taxed. But when the right to vote at any election for the choice of electors for President and Vice-President of the United States, Representatives in Congress, the Executive and Judicial officers of a State, or the members of the Legislature thereof, is denied to any of the male inhabitants of such State, being twenty-one years of age, and citizens of the United States, or in any way abridged, except for participation in rebellion, or other crime, the basis of representation therein shall be reduced in the proportion which the number of such male citizens shall bear to the whole number of male citizens twenty-one years of age in such State."

Section 3.

"No person shall be a Senator or Representative in Congress, or elector of President and Vice-President, or hold any office, civil or military, under the United States, or under any State, who, having previously taken an oath, as a member of Congress, or as an officer of the United States, or as a member of any State legislature, or as an executive or judicial officer of any State, to support the Constitution of the United States, shall have engaged in insurrection or rebellion against the same, or given aid or comfort to the enemies thereof. But Congress may by a vote of two-thirds of each House, remove such disability."

Section 4.

"The validity of the public debt of the United States, authorized by law, including debts incurred for payment of pensions and bounties for services in suppressing insurrection or rebellion, shall not be questioned. But neither the United States nor any State shall assume or pay any debt or obligation incurred in aid of insurrection or

rebellion against the United States, or any claim for the loss or emancipation of any slave; but all such debts, obligations and claims shall be held illegal and void."

Section 5.

"The Congress shall have power to enforce, by appropriate legislation, the provisions of this article."

Amendment XV (1870)

Right to Vote Not Denied by Race

Section 1.

"The right of citizens of the United States to vote shall not be denied or abridged by the United States or by any State on account of race, color, or previous condition of servitude."

Section 2.

"The Congress shall have power to enforce this article by appropriate legislation."

Amendment XVI (1913)

Income Tax

"The Congress shall have power to lay and collect taxes on incomes, from whatever source derived, without apportionment among the several States, and without regard to any census or enumeration."

Amendment XVII (1913)

Election of Senators by Popular Vote

"The Senate of the United States shall be composed of two Senators from each State, elected by the people thereof, for six years; and each Senator shall have one vote. The electors in each State shall have the qualifications requisite for electors of the most numerous branch of the State legislatures."

"When vacancies happen in the representation of any State in the Senate, the executive authority of such State shall issue writs of election to fill such vacancies: Provided, That the legislature of any State may empower the executive thereof to make temporary appointments until the people fill the vacancies by election as the legislature may direct."

"This amendment shall not be so construed as to affect the election or term of any Senator chosen before it becomes valid as part of the Constitution."

Amendment XVIII (1919)

Prohibition of Intoxicating Liquors

Section 1.

"After one year from the ratification of this article the manufacture, sale, or transportation of intoxicating liquors within, the importation thereof into, or the exportation thereof from the United States and all territory subject to the jurisdiction thereof for beverage purposes is hereby prohibited."

Section 2.

"The Congress and the several States shall have concurrent power to enforce this article by appropriate legislation."

Section 3.

"This article shall be inoperative unless it shall have been ratified as an amendment to the Constitution by the legislatures of the several States, as provided in the Constitution, within seven years from the date of the submission hereof to the States by the Congress."

Amendment XIX (1920)

Women's Right to Vote

"The right of citizens of the United States to vote shall not be denied or abridged by the United States or by any State on account of sex."

"Congress shall have power to enforce this article by appropriate legislation."

Amendment XX (1933)

Terms of the President and Congress

Section 1.

"The terms of the President and Vice President shall end at noon on the 20th day of January, and the terms of Senators and Representatives at noon on the 3rd day of January, of the years in which such terms would have ended if this article had not been ratified; and the terms of their successors shall then begin."

Section 2.

"The Congress shall assemble at least once in every year, and such meeting shall begin at noon on the 3rd day of January, unless they shall by law appoint a different day."

Section 3.

"If, at the time fixed for the beginning of the term of the President, the President-elect shall have died, the Vice President-elect shall become President. If a President shall not have been chosen before the time fixed for the beginning of his term, or if the President-elect shall have failed to qualify, then the Vice President-elect shall act as President until a President shall have qualified; and the Congress may by law provide for the case wherein neither a President-elect nor a Vice President-elect shall have qualified, declaring who shall then act as President, or the manner in which one who is to act shall be selected, and such person shall act accordingly until a President or Vice President shall have qualified."

Section 4.

"The Congress may by law provide for the case of the death of any of the persons from whom the House of Representatives may choose a President whenever the right of choice shall have devolved upon them, and for the case of the death of any of the persons from whom the Senate may choose a Vice President whenever the right of choice shall have devolved upon them."

Section 5.

"Sections 1 and 2 shall take effect on the 15th day of October following the ratification of this article."

Section 6.

"This article shall be inoperative unless it shall have been ratified as an amendment to the Constitution by the legislatures of three-fourths of the several States within seven years from the date of its submission."

Amendment XXI (1933)

Repeal of Prohibition

Section 1.

"The eighteenth article of amendment to the Constitution of the United States is hereby repealed."

Section 2.

"The transportation or importation into any State, Territory, or possession of the United States for delivery or use therein of intoxicating liquors, in violation of the laws thereof, is hereby prohibited."

Section 3.

"This article shall be inoperative unless it shall have been ratified as an amendment to the Constitution by conventions in the several States, as provided in the Constitution, within seven years from the date of the submission hereof to the States by the Congress."

Amendment XXII (1951)

Two-Term Limit on Presidency

Section 1.

"No person shall be elected to the office of the President more than twice, and no person who has held the office of President, or acted as President, for more than two years of a term to which some other person was elected President shall be elected to the office of President more than once. But this Article shall not apply to any person holding the office of President when this Article was proposed by the Congress, and shall not prevent any person who may be holding the office of President, or acting as President, during the term within which this Article becomes operative from holding the office of President or acting as President during the remainder of such term."

Section 2.

"This article shall be inoperative unless it shall have been ratified as an amendment to the Constitution by the legislatures of three-fourths of the several States within seven years from the date of its submission to the States by the Congress."

Amendment XXIII (1961)

Presidential Vote for D.C.

Section 1.

"The District constituting the seat of Government of the United States shall appoint in such manner as the Congress may direct:

* A number of electors of President and Vice President equal to the whole number of Senators and Representatives in Congress to which the District would be entitled if it were a State, but in no event more than the least populous State; they shall be in addition to those appointed by the States, but they shall be considered, for the purposes of the election of President and Vice President, to be electors appointed by a State; and they shall meet in the District and perform such duties as provided by the twelfth article of amendment."*

Section 2.

"The Congress shall have power to enforce this article by appropriate legislation."

Amendment XXIV (1964)

Abolition of Poll Taxes

Section 1.

"The right of citizens of the United States to vote in any primary or other election for President or Vice President, for electors for President or Vice President, or for Senator or Representative in Congress, shall not be denied or abridged by the United States or any State by reason of failure to pay any poll tax or other tax."

Section 2.

"The Congress shall have power to enforce this article by appropriate legislation."

Amendment XXV (1967)

Presidential Disability and Succession

Section 1.

"In case of the removal of the President from office or of his death or resignation, the Vice President shall become President."

Section 2.

"Whenever there is a vacancy in the office of the Vice President, the President shall nominate a Vice President who shall take office upon confirmation by a majority vote of both Houses of Congress."

Section 3.

"Whenever the President transmits to the President pro tempore of the Senate and the Speaker of the House of Representatives his written declaration that he is unable to discharge the powers and duties of his office, and until he transmits to them a written declaration to the contrary, such powers and duties shall be discharged by the Vice President as Acting President."

Section 4.

"Whenever the Vice President and a majority of either the principal officers of the executive departments or of such other body as Congress may by law provide, transmit to the President pro tempore of the Senate and the Speaker of the House of Representatives their written declaration that the President is unable to discharge the powers and duties of his office, the Vice President shall immediately assume the powers and duties of the office as Acting President.

Thereafter, when the President transmits to the President pro tempore of the Senate and the Speaker of the House of Representatives his written declaration that no inability exists, he shall resume the powers and duties of his office unless the Vice President and a majority of either the principal officers of the executive department or of such other body as Congress may by law provide, transmit within four days to the President pro tempore of the Senate and the Speaker of the House of Representatives their written declaration that the President is unable to discharge the powers and duties of his office. Thereupon Congress shall decide the issue, assembling within forty-eight hours for that purpose if not in session. If the Congress, within twenty-one days after receipt of the latter written declaration, or, if Congress is not in session, within twenty-one days after Congress is required to assemble, determines by two-thirds vote of both Houses that the President is unable to discharge the powers and duties of his office, the Vice President shall continue to discharge the same as Acting President; otherwise, the President shall resume the powers and duties of his office."

Amendment XXVI (1971)

Right to Vote at Age 18

Section 1.

"The right of citizens of the United States, who are eighteen years of age or older, to vote shall not be denied or abridged by the United States or by any State on account of age."

Section 2.

"The Congress shall have power to enforce this article by appropriate legislation."

Amendment XXVII (1992)

Congressional Pay Increases

"No law, varying the compensation for the services of the Senators and Representatives, shall take effect, until an election of Representatives shall have intervened."

Appendix C: Full Text of the Bill of Rights and Subsequent Amendments

The **United States Constitution** has been amended 27 times since its ratification in 1788. The first ten amendments, collectively known as the **Bill of Rights**, were ratified in 1791 and guarantee fundamental rights and protections to individuals. Subsequent amendments have addressed a range of issues, including the abolition of slavery, voting rights, and changes to governmental procedures. This appendix provides the full text of all 27 amendments, offering insight into the evolving principles and values of American democracy.

The Bill of Rights

Amendment I (1791)

Freedom of Religion, Speech, Press, Assembly, and Petition

"Congress shall make no law respecting an establishment of religion, or prohibiting the free exercise thereof; or abridging the freedom of speech, or of the press; or the right of the people peaceably to assemble, and to petition the Government for a redress of grievances."

Amendment II (1791)

Right to Keep and Bear Arms

"A well regulated Militia, being necessary to the security of a free State, the right of the people to keep and bear Arms, shall not be infringed."

Amendment III (1791)

Quartering of Soldiers

"No Soldier shall, in time of peace be quartered in any house, without the consent of the Owner, nor in time of war, but in a manner to be prescribed by law."

Amendment IV (1791)

Search and Seizure

"The right of the people to be secure in their persons, houses, papers, and effects, against unreasonable searches and seizures, shall not be violated, and no Warrants shall issue, but upon probable cause, supported by Oath or affirmation, and particularly describing the place to be searched, and the persons or things to be seized."

Amendment V (1791)

Rights in Criminal Cases

"No person shall be held to answer for a capital, or otherwise infamous crime, unless on a presentment or indictment of a Grand Jury, except in cases arising in the land or naval forces, or in the Militia, when in actual service in time of War or public danger; nor shall any person be subject for the same offence to be twice put in jeopardy of life or limb; nor shall be compelled in any criminal case to be a witness against himself, nor be deprived of life, liberty, or property, without due process of law; nor shall private property be taken for public use, without just compensation."

Amendment VI (1791)

Right to a Fair Trial

"In all criminal prosecutions, the accused shall enjoy the right to a speedy and public trial, by an impartial jury of the State and district wherein the crime shall have been committed, which district shall have been previously

ascertained by law, and to be informed of the nature and cause of the accusation; to be confronted with the witnesses against him; to have compulsory process for obtaining witnesses in his favor, and to have the Assistance of Counsel for his defence."

Amendment VII (1791)

Rights in Civil Cases

"In Suits at common law, where the value in controversy shall exceed twenty dollars, the right of trial by jury shall be preserved, and no fact tried by a jury, shall be otherwise re-examined in any Court of the United States, than according to the rules of the common law."

Amendment VIII (1791)

Bail, Fines, and Punishments

"Excessive bail shall not be required, nor excessive fines imposed, nor cruel and unusual punishments inflicted."

Amendment IX (1791)

Rights Retained by the People

"The enumeration in the Constitution, of certain rights, shall not be construed to deny or disparage others retained by the people."

Amendment X (1791)

States' Rights

"The powers not delegated to the United States by the Constitution, nor prohibited by it to the States, are reserved to the States respectively, or to the people."

Subsequent Amendments

Amendment XI (1795)

Lawsuits Against States

"The Judicial power of the United States shall not be construed to extend to any suit in law or equity, commenced or prosecuted against one of the United States by Citizens of another State, or by Citizens or Subjects of any Foreign State."

Amendment XII (1804)

Election of President and Vice President

"The Electors shall meet in their respective states and vote by ballot for President and Vice-President, one of whom, at least, shall not be an inhabitant of the same state with themselves; they shall name in their ballots the person voted for as President, and in distinct ballots the person voted for as Vice-President, and they shall make distinct lists of all persons voted for as President, and of all persons voted for as Vice-President, and of the number of votes for each, which lists they shall sign and certify, and transmit sealed to the seat of the government of the United States, directed to the President of the Senate;—The President of the Senate shall, in the presence of the Senate and House of Representatives, open all the certificates and the votes shall then be counted;—The person having the greatest number of votes for President, shall be the President, if such number be a majority of the whole number of Electors appointed; and if no person have such majority, then from the persons having the highest numbers not exceeding three on the list of those voted for as President, the House of Representatives shall choose immediately, by ballot, the President. But in choosing the President, the votes shall be taken by states, the representation from each state having one vote; a quorum for this purpose shall consist of a member

or members from two-thirds of the states, and a majority of all the states shall be necessary to a choice. And if the House of Representatives shall not choose a President whenever the right of choice shall devolve upon them, before the fourth day of March next following, then the Vice-President shall act as President, as in the case of the death or other constitutional disability of the President.—The person having the greatest number of votes as Vice-President, shall be the Vice-President, if such number be a majority of the whole number of Electors appointed, and if no person have a majority, then from the two highest numbers on the list, the Senate shall choose the Vice-President; a quorum for the purpose shall consist of two-thirds of the whole number of Senators, and a majority of the whole number shall be necessary to a choice. But no person constitutionally ineligible to the office of President shall be eligible to that of Vice-President of the United States."

Amendment XIII (1865)

Abolition of Slavery

Section 1.

"Neither slavery nor involuntary servitude, except as a punishment for crime whereof the party shall have been duly convicted, shall exist within the United States, or any place subject to their jurisdiction."

Section 2.

"Congress shall have power to enforce this article by appropriate legislation."

Amendment XIV (1868)

Citizenship, Due Process, and Equal Protection

Section 1.

"All persons born or naturalized in the United States, and subject to the jurisdiction thereof, are citizens of the United States and of the State wherein they reside. No State shall make or enforce any law which shall abridge the privileges or immunities of citizens of the United States; nor shall any State deprive any person of life, liberty, or property, without due process of law; nor deny to any person within its jurisdiction the equal protection of the laws."

Section 2.

"Representatives shall be apportioned among the several States according to their respective numbers, counting the whole number of persons in each State, excluding Indians not taxed. But when the right to vote at any election for the choice of electors for President and Vice-President of the United States, Representatives in Congress, the Executive and Judicial officers of a State, or the members of the Legislature thereof, is denied to any of the male inhabitants of such State, being twenty-one years of age, and citizens of the United States, or in any way abridged, except for participation in rebellion, or other crime, the basis of representation therein shall be reduced in the proportion which the number of such male citizens shall bear to the whole number of male citizens twenty-one years of age in such State."

Section 3.

"No person shall be a Senator or Representative in Congress, or elector of President and Vice-President, or hold any office, civil or military, under the United States, or under any State, who, having previously taken an oath, as a member of Congress, or as an officer of the United States, or as a member of any State legislature, or as an executive or judicial officer of any State, to support the Constitution of the United States, shall have engaged in insurrection or rebellion against the same, or given aid or comfort to the enemies thereof. But Congress may by a vote of two-thirds of each House, remove such disability."

Section 4.

"The validity of the public debt of the United States, authorized by law, including debts incurred for payment of pensions and bounties for services in suppressing insurrection or rebellion, shall not be questioned. But neither the United States nor any State shall assume or pay any debt or obligation incurred in aid of insurrection or rebellion against the United States, or any claim for the loss or emancipation of any slave; but all such debts, obligations and claims shall be held illegal and void."

Section 5.

"The Congress shall have power to enforce, by appropriate legislation, the provisions of this article."

Amendment XV (1870)

Right to Vote Not Denied by Race

Section 1.

"The right of citizens of the United States to vote shall not be denied or abridged by the United States or by any State on account of race, color, or previous condition of servitude."

Section 2.

"The Congress shall have power to enforce this article by appropriate legislation."

Amendment XVI (1913)

Income Tax

"The Congress shall have power to lay and collect taxes on incomes, from whatever source derived, without apportionment among the several States, and without regard to any census or enumeration."

Amendment XVII (1913)

Election of Senators by Popular Vote

"The Senate of the United States shall be composed of two Senators from each State, elected by the people thereof, for six years; and each Senator shall have one vote. The electors in each State shall have the qualifications requisite for electors of the most numerous branch of the State legislatures."

"When vacancies happen in the representation of any State in the Senate, the executive authority of such State shall issue writs of election to fill such vacancies: Provided, That the legislature of any State may empower the executive thereof to make temporary appointments until the people fill the vacancies by election as the legislature may direct."

"This amendment shall not be so construed as to affect the election or term of any Senator chosen before it becomes valid as part of the Constitution."

Amendment XVIII (1919)

Prohibition of Intoxicating Liquors

Section 1.

"After one year from the ratification of this article the manufacture, sale, or transportation of intoxicating liquors within, the importation thereof into, or the exportation thereof from the United States and all territory subject to the jurisdiction thereof for beverage purposes is hereby prohibited."

Section 2.

"The Congress and the several States shall have concurrent power to enforce this article by appropriate legislation."

Section 3.

"This article shall be inoperative unless it shall have been ratified as an amendment to the Constitution by the legislatures of the several States, as provided in the Constitution, within seven years from the date of the submission hereof to the States by the Congress."

Amendment XIX (1920)

Women's Right to Vote

"The right of citizens of the United States to vote shall not be denied or abridged by the United States or by any State on account of sex."

"Congress shall have power to enforce this article by appropriate legislation."

Amendment XX (1933)

Terms of the President and Congress

Section 1.

"The terms of the President and Vice President shall end at noon on the 20th day of January, and the terms of Senators and Representatives at noon on the 3rd day of January, of the years in which such terms would have ended if this article had not been ratified; and the terms of their successors shall then begin."

Section 2.

"The Congress shall assemble at least once in every year, and such meeting shall begin at noon on the 3rd day of January, unless they shall by law appoint a different day."

Section 3.

"If, at the time fixed for the beginning of the term of the President, the President-elect shall have died, the Vice President-elect shall become President. If a President shall not have been chosen before the time fixed for the beginning of his term, or if the President-elect shall have failed to qualify, then the Vice President-elect shall act as President until a President shall have qualified; and the Congress may by law provide for the case wherein neither a President-elect nor a Vice President-elect shall have qualified, declaring who shall then act as President, or the manner in which one who is to act shall be selected, and such person shall act accordingly until a President or Vice President shall have qualified."

Section 4.

"The Congress may by law provide for the case of the death of any of the persons from whom the House of Representatives may choose a President whenever the right of choice shall devolve upon them, and for the case of the death of any of the persons from whom the Senate may choose a Vice President whenever the right of choice shall devolve upon them."

Section 5.

"Sections 1 and 2 shall take effect on the 15th day of October following the ratification of this article."

Section 6.

"This article shall be inoperative unless it shall have been ratified as an amendment to the Constitution by the legislatures of three-fourths of the several States within seven years from the date of its submission."

Amendment XXI (1933)

Repeal of Prohibition

Section 1.

"The eighteenth article of amendment to the Constitution of the United States is hereby repealed."

Section 2.

"The transportation or importation into any State, Territory, or possession of the United States for delivery or use therein of intoxicating liquors, in violation of the laws thereof, is hereby prohibited."

Section 3.

"This article shall be inoperative unless it shall have been ratified as an amendment to the Constitution by conventions in the several States, as provided in the Constitution, within seven years from the date of the submission hereof to the States by the Congress."

Amendment XXII (1951)

Two-Term Limit on Presidency

Section 1.

"No person shall be elected to the office of the President more than twice, and no person who has held the office of President, or acted as President, for more than two years of a term to which some other person was elected President shall be elected to the office of President more than once. But this Article shall not apply to any person holding the office of President when this Article was proposed by the Congress, and shall not prevent any person who may be holding the office of President, or acting as President, during the term within which this Article becomes operative from holding the office of President or acting as President during the remainder of such term."

Section 2.

"This article shall be inoperative unless it shall have been ratified as an amendment to the Constitution by the legislatures of three-fourths of the several States within seven years from the date of its submission to the States by the Congress."

Amendment XXIII (1961)

Presidential Vote for the District of Columbia

Section 1.

"The District constituting the seat of Government of the United States shall appoint in such manner as the Congress may direct:

* A number of electors of President and Vice President equal to the whole number of Senators and Representatives in Congress to which the District would be entitled if it were a State, but in no event more than the least populous State; they shall be in addition to those appointed by the States, but they shall be considered, for the purposes of the election of President and Vice President, to be electors appointed by a State; and they shall meet in the District and perform such duties as provided by the twelfth article of amendment."*

Section 2.

"The Congress shall have power to enforce this article by appropriate legislation."

Amendment XXIV (1964)

Abolition of Poll Taxes

Section 1.

"The right of citizens of the United States to vote in any primary or other election for President or Vice President, for electors for President or Vice President, or for Senator or Representative in Congress, shall not be denied or abridged by the United States or any State by reason of failure to pay any poll tax or other tax."

Section 2.

"The Congress shall have power to enforce this article by appropriate legislation."

Amendment XXV (1967)

Presidential Disability and Succession

Section 1.

"In case of the removal of the President from office or of his death or resignation, the Vice President shall become President."

Section 2.

"Whenever there is a vacancy in the office of the Vice President, the President shall nominate a Vice President who shall take office upon confirmation by a majority vote of both Houses of Congress."

Section 3.

"Whenever the President transmits to the President pro tempore of the Senate and the Speaker of the House of Representatives his written declaration that he is unable to discharge the powers and duties of his office, and until he transmits to them a written declaration to the contrary, such powers and duties shall be discharged by the Vice President as Acting President."

Section 4.

"Whenever the Vice President and a majority of either the principal officers of the executive departments or of such other body as Congress may by law provide, transmit to the President pro tempore of the Senate and the Speaker of the House of Representatives their written declaration that the President is unable to discharge the powers and duties of his office, the Vice President shall immediately assume the powers and duties of the office as Acting President.

Thereafter, when the President transmits to the President pro tempore of the Senate and the Speaker of the House of Representatives his written declaration that no inability exists, he shall resume the powers and duties of his office unless the Vice President and a majority of either the principal officers of the executive departments or of such other body as Congress may by law provide, transmit within four days to the President pro tempore of the Senate and the Speaker of the House of Representatives their written declaration that the President is unable to discharge the powers and duties of his office. Thereupon Congress shall decide the issue, assembling within forty-eight hours for that purpose if not in session. If the Congress, within twenty-one days after receipt of the latter written declaration, or, if Congress is not in session, within twenty-one days after Congress is required to assemble, determines by two-thirds vote of both Houses that the President is unable to discharge the powers and duties of his office, the Vice President shall continue to discharge the same as Acting President; otherwise, the President shall resume the powers and duties of his office."

Amendment XXVI (1971)

Right to Vote at Age 18

Section 1.

"The right of citizens of the United States, who are eighteen years of age or older, to vote shall not be denied or abridged by the United States or by any State on account of age."

Section 2.

"The Congress shall have power to enforce this article by appropriate legislation."

Amendment XXVII (1992)

Congressional Pay Increases

"No law, varying the compensation for the services of the Senators and Representatives, shall take effect, until an election of Representatives shall have intervened."

Appendix D: Selected Federalist and Anti-Federalist Papers

The **Federalist Papers** and the **Anti-Federalist Papers** are seminal works in American political history. Written during the critical period of debate over the ratification of the United States Constitution, these essays provide deep insights into the foundational ideas and concerns that shaped the nation's government. The Federalist Papers advocated for the Constitution's adoption, highlighting the need for a strong central government, while the Anti-Federalist Papers expressed concerns over potential threats to individual liberties and state sovereignty.

This appendix presents selected essays from both collections, offering a balanced perspective on the arguments that influenced the formation of the U.S. Constitution. By studying these documents, readers can gain a deeper understanding of the principles, debates, and compromises that have had a lasting impact on American governance.

Selected Federalist Papers

Federalist No. 10

Author: James Madison

Title: *The Utility of the Union as a Safeguard Against Domestic Faction and Insurrection*

To the People of the State of New York:

Among the numerous advantages promised by a well-constructed Union, none deserves to be more accurately developed than its tendency to break and control the violence of faction. The friend of popular governments never finds himself so much alarmed for their character and fate as when he contemplates their propensity to this dangerous vice.

By a faction, I understand a number of citizens, whether amounting to a majority or a minority of the whole, who are united and actuated by some common impulse of passion or of interest adverse to the rights of other citizens or to the permanent and aggregate interests of the community.

The Causes of Faction

There are two methods of curing the mischiefs of faction: the one, by removing its causes; the other, by controlling its effects.

1. **Removing Its Causes**
    - **Destroying Liberty**: Liberty is to faction what air is to fire. But abolishing liberty is a remedy worse than the disease.
    - **Uniformity of Opinions**: The diversity in the faculties of men, from which the rights of property originate, is an insuperable obstacle to uniformity.
2. **Controlling Its Effects**
    - **A Republic vs. Pure Democracy**: A republic can refine and enlarge public views by passing them through a medium of a chosen body of citizens.

The Advantage of a Large Republic

In a large republic, a variety of interests and parties makes it less probable that a majority will have a common motive to invade the rights of other citizens.

Federalist No. 51

Author: James Madison

Title: *The Structure of the Government Must Furnish the Proper Checks and Balances Between the Different Departments*

To the People of the State of New York:

To what expedient, then, shall we finally resort for maintaining in practice the necessary partition of power among the several departments as laid down in the Constitution?

Separation of Powers

- Each department should have a will of its own.
- Members of each should have as little agency as possible in the appointment of the members of the others.
- The great security lies in giving those who administer each department the necessary constitutional means and personal motives to resist encroachments.

Checks and Balances

- Ambition must be made to counteract ambition.
- The interest of the man must be connected with the constitutional rights of the place.

Justice as the End

Justice is the end of government. It is the end of civil society. It ever has been and ever will be pursued until it is obtained or until liberty is lost in the pursuit.

Federalist No. 78

Author: Alexander Hamilton

Title: *The Judiciary Department*

To the People of the State of New York:

The judiciary is beyond comparison the weakest of the three departments of power.

Judicial Independence

- The judiciary has no influence over either the sword or the purse.
- It must depend upon the aid of the executive arm for the efficacy of its judgments.

Permanent Tenure

- The independence of judges is essential to guard the Constitution and the rights of individuals from the effects of ill humors in society.
- Permanent tenure is necessary to attract men of virtue and abilities.

Judicial Review

- It is the duty of the judiciary to declare all acts contrary to the manifest tenor of the Constitution void.
- Courts are to interpret the laws and ensure that no legislative act contrary to the Constitution is valid.

Selected Anti-Federalist Papers

Brutus No. 1

Author: Robert Yates (attributed)

Title: *Questions the Viability of a Large Republic*

When the public is called to investigate and decide upon a question in which not only the present members of the community are deeply interested, but upon which the happiness and misery of generations yet unborn is in great measure suspended, the benevolent mind cannot help feeling itself peculiarly interested.

Concerns Over Centralized Power

- A large republic cannot adequately represent the interests of its citizens.
- The necessary and proper clause and the supremacy clause grant too much power to the federal government.

The Fate of Free Republics

- History shows that free republics have always ended in tyranny when they become too large.
- The vast territory of the United States makes it impractical to govern effectively without resorting to despotism.

Cato No. 3

Author: Possibly George Clinton

Title: *Critiques the Executive Branch*

The most important part of the constitution of a government is the organization of the legislative and executive departments.

Fear of an Energetic Executive

- The proposed executive is granted powers that may lead to monarchy.
- The absence of a council to check the executive's power is dangerous.

Term Length and Re-Eligibility

- The four-year term with the possibility of indefinite re-election may encourage the president to consolidate power.
- Rotation in office is necessary to prevent the rise of an entrenched ruling class.

Federal Farmer No. 1

Author: Possibly Richard Henry Lee

Title: *Advocates for a Federal System with Strong State Governments*

Dear Sir,

The plan of government now proposed is evidently calculated totally to change, in time, our condition as a people.

The Importance of State Sovereignty

- State governments are closer to the people and better understand their needs.
- Consolidation of power in a central government poses risks to liberty.

Representation Concerns

- The proposed House of Representatives is too small to represent the diverse interests of the populace adequately.
- Frequent elections and a larger number of representatives are necessary to keep the government accountable.

Significance of the Federalist and Anti-Federalist Papers

The Federalist and Anti-Federalist Papers played a crucial role in shaping the debate over the ratification of the U.S. Constitution.

- **Federalist Papers**: Written by Alexander Hamilton, James Madison, and John Jay under the pseudonym "Publius," these essays argued in favor of the new Constitution. They explained the need for a stronger central government and addressed concerns about the potential for tyranny by emphasizing the system of checks and balances.
- **Anti-Federalist Papers**: Composed by various authors using pseudonyms like "Brutus," "Cato," and "Federal Farmer," these writings expressed skepticism about the proposed Constitution. They feared that a strong central government would infringe on the rights of states and individuals and argued for the inclusion of a bill of rights.

Key Themes in the Debate:

1. **Size and Scope of Government**: Anti-Federalists were concerned that the vast geography of the United States would make it difficult for a central government to represent the people's interests effectively.
2. **Representation**: Questions were raised about whether the proposed legislative structures would adequately reflect the will of the people.
3. **Checks and Balances**: Federalists emphasized the mechanisms within the Constitution designed to prevent any one branch from becoming too powerful.
4. **Individual Rights**: The lack of a bill of rights in the original Constitution was a significant point of contention, leading to the eventual adoption of the first ten amendments.

Impact on the Constitution:

- The **Bill of Rights**: The Anti-Federalists' insistence on protecting individual liberties resulted in the first ten amendments to the Constitution, ensuring fundamental rights such as freedom of speech, religion, and due process.
- **Federal Structure**: The debates highlighted the importance of balancing power between the national and state governments, shaping federalism in the United States.

Made in United States
Orlando, FL
02 April 2025